Cast On, Bind Off

211 Ways to Begin and End Your Knitting

Cap Sease

Martingale®
Create with Confidence

Dedication

*To my grandmother Lenore Lieurance,
who taught me my first cast on and bind off.*

Cast On, Bind Off:
211 Ways to Begin and End Your Knitting
© 2012 by Catherine Sease

Martingale®
19021 120th Ave. NE, Ste. 102
Bothell, WA 98011-9511 USA
ShopMartingale.com

Printed in China
19 18 17 16 15 14   8 7 6 5 4 3 2 1

**Library of Congress Cataloging-in-Publication Data
is available upon request.**

ISBN: 978-1-60468-429-2

Mission Statement

*Dedicated to providing quality products
and service to inspire creativity.*

Credits

President & CEO: Tom Wierzbicki

Editor in Chief: Mary V. Green

Design Director: Paula Schlosser

Managing Editor: Karen Costello Soltys

Technical Editor: Ursula Reikes

Copy Editor: Melissa Bryan

Production Manager: Regina Girard

Text & Cover Designer: Regina Girard

Illustrators: Laurel Strand, Robin Strobel

Photographer: Brent Kane

Contents

Introduction

The tremendous diversity in knitting makes it a wonderful, creative process. Casting on and binding off are no exceptions. Both procedures can be performed in an astonishing number of ways, each creating an edge with its own particular characteristics and look.

This creativity has also led to confusion. Sometimes, structurally different cast ons have the same name, while other cast ons that are quite similar are referred to by numerous different names. Frequently, I think I've come upon a new cast-on technique, only to find that I already have it in my repertoire but with a different name. Just leafing through a few pages of this book, you can see how similar many of the names are and how often the same names are used.

In addition, the different types of cast ons are often mixed up with each other, especially the tubular and provisional cast ons and bind offs. These terms are often used interchangeably, but in fact they are two very different techniques to be used for very different purposes.

I've tried to make sense out of this confusion by sorting the cast ons and bind offs into groups according to the way they're worked, the edges they produce, or their function. This is easier to do for the cast ons than the bind offs, but they too can be grouped, at least loosely, by similar construction techniques.

In presenting the techniques here, I used the name I found to be the one most commonly used for each technique. Less common, alternate names are included in an "also called" category.

Many techniques have one or more variations. If the differences are minor and are just a different way to produce the same edge, I've described them as variations and included them under the main technique. If the variation is sufficiently different, I have distinguished it through its own name and description. Although these divisions are subjective decisions on my part, I hope they will help to clear up some confusion and make things easier for you.

The extraordinary number of different ways to cast on and bind off is a tribute to the ingenuity and creativity of knitters. I hope this book will be a useful reference that encourages knitters to experiment and find new ways to enhance their wonderful creations. Enjoy!

How to Choose a Cast On or Bind Off

There is no right or wrong way to cast on or bind off. Each technique has its own look and characteristics, which may be just right for some applications and not suitable for others.

In choosing which to use, you need to keep several things in mind. Function is probably the most important consideration. What's the purpose of the edge and how will it be used? Will it be subjected to considerable wear and tear on a child's sweater or hat, or will it be on a shawl that won't be used quite so heavily? The bottoms of sweaters, especially on pullovers, need to be stretchy enough to allow them to be pulled on over the head. Neckbands, hat bands, and sock cuffs also need to be elastic in order to serve their proper function. Lace patterns, especially those that produce scalloped or serrated edges, require flexible edges to realize their full potential. Most of the long-tail cast ons and the chain bind offs would be suitable for any of these items.

Other projects, however, benefit from firmer, less flexible edges. You might want the edges of pockets and bags or the brim of some hats to be firm to keep them from stretching and becoming floppy. In this instance, the cable cast on might be a good choice.

Aesthetics are also an important consideration. What do you want the edge to look like? Will it be hidden in a seam where looks won't matter, or will it be visible? If the latter, do you want it to be a design element? Any of the cast ons and bind offs in the decorative sections would add a distinctive look to your work. By becoming familiar with a variety of techniques, you can choose the look that will enhance your project and add to the overall effect.

If you're working in ribbing, especially K1, P1 ribbing, and you like the look of the invisible rounded edge on commercial knitwear, a tubular cast on and bind off could be the perfect choice. If it's important for the bound-off edge to look just like the cast-on edge, for example on a scarf or shawl, you can choose a pair of techniques that produce the same edge.

The choice of a cast on or bind off might also depend on your pattern stitch. A picot edge can set off the lace pattern in a shawl or add a distinctive touch to ribbing, as with the picot ribbing cast on.

And certainly an important consideration in your choice is how comfortable you are with working the technique. Every knitter finds certain techniques easier to work than others. Most students I've taught find the German Twisted cast on difficult to do, but if that's the edge you want, there are different ways to work it. For example, the Maine, English, and Twisted Italian cast ons produce the same edge, and you may find one of these easier to work. The variations of the different techniques presented here, although not all simple or easy to execute, should provide you with at least one way to produce the edge that you want.

The following tables may help you find the right cast on or bind off for your next project.

Cast Ons

Purpose	Methods (page numbers are indicated in parentheses)
Adding Stitches in Mid-Project	Backward-Loop (14), Buttonhole (92), Cable (51), Chained (64), Crochet Chain (92), Knit (48), Loop (13), Purled (50), Purl Cable (52)
All-Around	Double-Needle (46), English (37), German Twisted (34), Knit (48), Left-Handed (29), Long-Tail (18), Purled (50), Purled Half-Hitch (31), Simplified (28), Two-Needle (30)
Brioche Stitch	Two-Strand Tubular (82)
Corrugated Ribbing	German Twisted (34)
Durable	Channel Island (42), Combined Long-Tail: Thick Variation (27), Double Long-Tail (21), Knit (48), Knotted (45), Long-Tail (18), Purled (50), Triple Long-Tail (23)
Elastic	Austrian (40), Chain (63), Chained (64), Channel Island (42), Double-Needle (46), Double-Twist (39), English (37), German Twisted (34), Knit (48), Knotted (45), Lace (98), Long-Tail (18), Picot (69), Picot Chain (70), Slipknot (73), all Tubulars (75), Twisted Italian (36), Twisted-Loop (16)
Firm, Nonelastic Edge	Alternate Cable (53), Cable (51), Chain (63), Double Long-Tail (21), Knit (48), Purled (50), Triple Long-Tail (23)
Garter Stitch	Channel Island (42), Double (74), Double Twist (39), English (37), German Twisted (34), Knotted (45), Picot (69), Thumb (41), Twisted Italian (36)
Hemmed Edge	Backward-Loop (14), Chain (63), Loop (13), Twisted-Loop (16)
Lace	Alternate-Loop (15), Chain (63), Chained Variation (64), Double-Needle (46), Edging (66), Knit (48), Lace (98), Loop (13), Picot (69), Picot Chain (70), Twisted-Loop (16)
Noncurling Edges	Austrian (40), English (37), German Twisted (34), all Tubulars (75), Twice-Knitted (49), Twisted Italian (36)
Novelty Yarns	Alternate-Loop (15), Backward-Loop (14), Loop (13)
Reversible (identical on both sides)	Backward-Loop (14), Cable (51), Chinese Waitress (54), Double (74), Kihnu Troi (59), Loop (13), Slipknot (73)
Ribbing	Alternate Cable (53), Channel Island (42), Frilled (61), German Twisted (34), K1, P1 Rib (32), Knit-Purl (50), all Long-Tail (18), Picot (69), Picot Ribbing (72), all Tubulars (75)
Rolled Edge	Backward-Loop (14), Basic Long-Tail: in Stockinette (18), Cable: in Stockinette (51), Chain (63), Knit: in Stockinette (48), Loop (13)
Socks	Backward-Loop Sock (106), Closed-Toe (108), Easy Toe (110), Figure-Eight Wrap (105), Judy's Magic (107), Patti's Closed-Toe Crochet Chain (111), Rolled-Edge (102), Straight Wrap (104), The Best Toe-Up for Magic Loop (109)

Bind Offs

Purpose	Methods (page numbers are indicated in parentheses)
All-Around	Crochet (115), Decrease (123), Russian (119), Standard (114)
Brioche Stitch	Invisible Ribbed (153), Simple Two-Color (124)
Buttonholes	K2tog (124), Without Knitting (114)
Durable	All Chains (114), Cowichan Double (142), Decrease (123), Double-Stranded (144), Japanese (136), K2tog (124), Russian Grafting (139), Simple Two-Color (124), Slanted (136), Stem-Stitch (146), Three-Needle (137), Zigzag (141)
Elastic	Decrease (123), Double-Crochet (116), Elastic (123), all Increases (131), Jeny's Surprisingly Stretchy (135), Latvian (145), Peggy's Stretchy (133), Picot Chain (132), Ribbing (118), Russian (119), Sarah's Favorite (132), Sewn (144), Stretchy (121), Suspended (120), all Tubulars (150), Yarn-Over (134)
Firm, Nonelastic Edge	Braided-Rib (116), Double-Stitch (117), Double-Stranded (144), K2tog (124), One-Over-Two (117), Two-Row (122), Without Knitting (114)
Joining Pieces	Cowichan Double (142), Japanese (136), Kitchener (148), Russian Grafting (139), Three-Needle (137), Three-Needle I-Cord (138), Zigzag (141)
Lace	Crown Picot (129), Edging (126), Long-Chain (130), all Picots (126), Picot Chain (132), Suspended (120), Yarn-Over (134)
Novelty Yarns	Crochet (115)
Ribbing	Cable (118), Decrease (123), Elastic (123), Jeny's Surprisingly Stretchy (135), Peggy's Stretchy (133), Ribbing (118), Sarah's Favorite (132), Stretchy (121), all Tubulars (150), Two-Row (122), Yarn-Over (134)

Cast-On and Bind-Off Pairs

Pair the following cast ons and bind offs to create matching edges.

Cast Ons	Bind Offs
Chain Cast On (63)	Standard Bind Off (114)
Edging Cast On (66)	Edging Bind Off (126)
I-Cord Cast On (65)	I-Cord Bind Off (125)
Long-Tail Cast On (18)	Sewn Bind Off (144)
Long-Tail Cast On (18)	Stem-Stitch Bind Off (146)
Long-Tail Cast On (18)	Standard Bind Off (114)
Loop Cast On (13)	Loop Bind Off (147)
Picot Cast Ons (69)	Picot Bind Offs (126)
Tubular Cast Ons (75)	Tubular Bind Offs (150)

It All Starts with Casting On

Casting on is the procedure used to put loops, or stitches, onto a needle so that you can knit. It's the foundation of hand knitting and the beginning of every individual piece you knit. In fact, in old knitting books casting on was called "setting up the foundation." There are a surprising number of ways to cast on and start a project. Most knitters, however, use only the method they were taught when they first learned to knit, and are not aware of the number and diversity of cast-on techniques available.

Each cast on has advantages and disadvantages that make it appropriate for some applications and not for others. Some produce firm edges suitable for mats, rugs, and certain garments; others produce elastic edges ideal for hats, socks, and sweaters; and even others create almost no discernable edge at all. Many create decorative edges that add different effects and can be used as design elements to personalize your work. Others are functional and temporary, allowing you to get your project started and later turn around and work in the opposite direction, which can be very useful when you want both ends of a scarf or shawl, for example, to be exactly the same. Or, when you knit socks, you can choose from several cast ons allowing you to start from the toe or at the cuff edge. Whatever your project, there's at least one cast on that will be ideal for the job and add style to your work.

I recommend becoming familiar with several techniques so that you can create the proper qualities and effects for each situation. Choosing the right cast on is just one of the many details that can influence what your finished project will look like, and also how it will wear. The wrong choice can detract from all the hard work you will put into your piece. A cast-on edge that is too tight or rigid can make a sweater, for example, hard to put on. This in turn will strain the yarn along the cast-on edge, causing it to wear poorly and break. It can also cause the knitting above the edge to pucker or bulge out. On the other hand, a cast-on edge that is too loose will be floppy and make your garment flare out at the bottom rather than fit well.

Your choice of yarn may also dictate your choice of cast on. Since wool is resilient, it works well with any flexible cast on. Less elastic, resilient yarns, such as cotton, silk, and many synthetics, generally work better with a firmer cast on.

You will find a wide variety of cast-on techniques presented here. Experiment with them to see what effects they create. Once you become familiar with them, you'll find many new ways to enhance and professionalize your knitting.

The cast ons are grouped into families (starting on page 12) based on similar construction or use.

Tips for Casting On

Everyone knits differently. Although patterns call for a needle of a certain size, you may find that you cast on more tightly or loosely than the project specifies.

If your cast-on stitches are too tight, many people recommend casting on with needles one or two sizes larger than the needles called for in the pattern. Doing this does loosen the stitches, but it can also cause the first row of stitches to be elongated and look different from the rest of your knitting. It can be more effective to space the stitches farther apart on the needle as you cast on. This will give you a little extra yarn, allowing the stitches to become slightly bigger when knitting the first row.

If your cast-on stitches are too loose, you can try using needles a size or two smaller. But make sure you don't overcompensate and make your stitches too tight. You can also try to space the stitches closer together on the needle as you cast on.

Most cast ons start with a slipknot (page 10). Although the knots generally end up in the seam of your garment where they don't show, many people simply do not like slipknots in their knitting. If you're in this group, choose a method such as a loop, knit, or cable cast on where the knot is at the beginning of the row of stitches. After casting on, you can undo the knot and easily remove it from the needle. However, there are many methods for which this won't work, including the long-tail cast ons. For these, you can use the twist start technique (page 11).

If you're going to knit cables within a few rows of casting on, you may find that the cables pull in, causing the edge to flare out below the cables. You can avoid this by casting on a stitch or two less under each cable. After a row or two, but before you twist the cable, increase up to the correct number of stitches in the middle of the cable. The increases will not show and the edge of the knitting should remain flat.

Slipknots

Most cast ons start with a slipknot. This is a simple knot that places and secures the yarn on the needle, enabling you to cast on. Usually the knot counts as the first stitch, but sometimes it's merely used to stabilize the yarn for the cast on. In that instance, after several rows have been worked, the knot is untied and the ends are woven in.

Here are just a few of the many ways to make a slipknot.

Slipknot 1

Make a loop in the yarn where you want the slipknot to be, with the tail strand on top of the ball strand. Bring the tail strand behind the loop and pull it through the loop with the needle. Pull both strands to tighten the knot on the needle.

Slipknot 2

1. Hold the yarn taut between the fingers of both hands with the tail on the left and the ball on the right. Wrap the yarn up and over the left thumb and index finger.

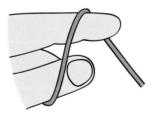

2. Rotate your left hand to the right, away from you, to create a loop around the index finger. With the right thumb and index finger, pinch where the two strands cross, just above the left thumb.

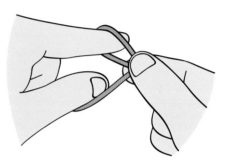

3. Crook the left index finger and bring its tip in front of the thumb strand, then down and under the strand and up to catch it. Pull the strand through the loop.

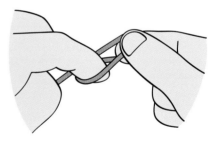

4. Pull the ball strand to tighten the loop. Place the loop on the needle.

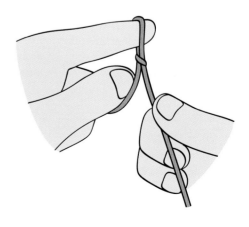

Slipknot 3

1. Extend the left index and middle fingers. Holding the tail in the last two fingers of the left hand, wrap the yarn around the extended fingers from front to back, starting at the top of the index finger. When you reach the front of the index finger again, cross over the first wrap and bring the strand over the index finger to the left of the first wrap, letting the strand hang loosely in back.

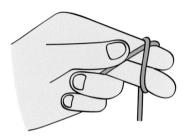

2. Insert the needle into the loop around the fingers from the right, catch the hanging back strand, and pull it through the loop. Remove the fingers from the loops and pull the strands to tighten the knot.

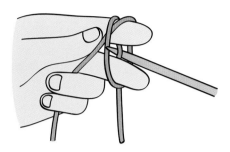

Twist Start

Some knitters prefer casting on without slipknots. In this technique, the yarn is simply wrapped around the needle, creating what some feel is a neater end to the cast-on edge. The twist start cannot be used for the knit cast ons, but it works well with the long-tail options.

Twist Start

1. Leaving a long tail, wrap the yarn around the left thumb and index finger, with the tail on the left and the working strand on the right. Hold both ends in the remaining fingers of your left hand.

2. Point the needle downward behind the strand stretching between the thumb and index finger.

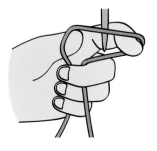

3. Hold the needle against the strand while rotating the needle clockwise until the tip points up.

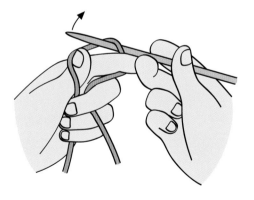

4. A loop has now been created on the needle. Place your right index finger on the loop to keep it in place, and then start to cast on through the thumb loop as described for your chosen cast-on method.

Twist Start Variation

1. Wrap the yarn around the left thumb and index finger, with the tail over the thumb and the working end over the index finger. Hold both tails in the remaining fingers of your left hand.

2. Place the needle under the strand between the thumb and index finger.

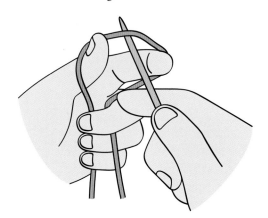

3. Lift the needle slightly against the strand and rotate it clockwise 360°.

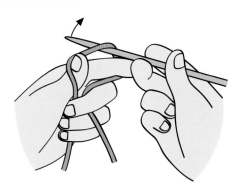

4. A twisted loop has now been created on the needle. Start to cast on through the thumb loop as described for your chosen cast-on method. The extra twist can make the last stitch looser than the rest of the stitches. To correct this, knit in the back of this stitch on the first row of knitting.

Loop Cast Ons

The loop methods are the least complicated options for casting on. Because they are easy to understand, they are often the first cast ons taught to beginners. However, although not complex, they're not necessarily the easiest to do well. As you pull the right needle to insert it into the stitch to knit, the strand is pulled tight, making the first stitch hard to get the needle into. The more you try to pull, the tighter it gets. Unless worked carefully, the edges tend to be uneven, loose, and sometimes sloppy. While the tension can be adjusted once the stitches are on the needle, this is a fussy job. Also, the first row of knitting can be difficult to execute because the tension changes as you work the stitches.

As a result, these cast ons are best used when you require only a small number of stitches. The loop, backward-loop, and alternate-loop cast ons produce results that have only one strand of yarn along the edge, and therefore, they do not wear as well as other cast-on edges.

Because they are not intricate and involve a minimal amount of yarn manipulation, these cast ons work well with novelty yarns, which tend to be delicate and easily frayed. Pair this cast on with the loop bind off (page 147) for matching edges.

With all of the loop cast ons, there is a tendency for the strand between the stitches to lengthen as you work the first row. To minimize this, insert the right needle all the way up to its shaft into the loop on the left needle, rather than inserting just the tip of the needle into the loop. Before knitting the stitch, gently pull the loop with the right needle to open it up, and then knit the stitch.

Loop Cast On

Also called Simple Cast On, Simple Looped Cast On, Single Cast On, Purl Loop Cast On, E-Wrap Cast On, Left-Slanting Loop Cast On

This cast on produces an edge that is loose and tends to flare, so there are many projects for which it is not appropriate. It can be used successfully for lace and is well suited to adding stitches in the middle of a project, such as for steeks or when the cast-on edges will be hidden in a seam. Since there is no bulk, it's a good choice for edges that will be seamed. It also adapts nicely to rolled edges, allowing them to curl while keeping the loose edges out of sight. You may also use this cast on for buttonholes, but make sure you work it tightly.

For a firmer edge, knit through the back of the stitches on the first row only. This will alter the look of the edge as the stitches are twisted.

Loop cast on

Loop cast on, knit through the back loop on first row

1. With the needle in the left hand, hold the yarn taut between both hands with the tail on the left and the ball on the right.

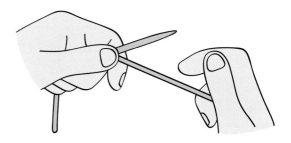

2. *Swing the right thumb over, behind, and under the yarn, and then up to create a loop on the thumb.

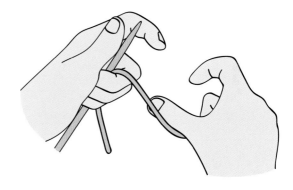

3. Bending the thumb slightly away from you, insert the needle into the thumb loop as if to knit.

4. Remove the thumb and pull the yarn to tighten the stitch. Repeat from *.

Loop Cast On Variation

1. Make a slipknot about 5" from the end of the yarn and place it on the needle. Hold the needle in the left hand and hold the yarn taut in the right fingers.

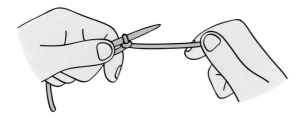

2. Swing the right index finger behind and under the yarn, and then forward and up to wrap the yarn around the finger.

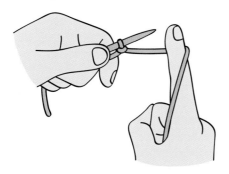

3. Rotate the finger clockwise to create a loop on the finger, insert the needle into the loop from left to right, remove the finger, and tighten the stitch on the needle.

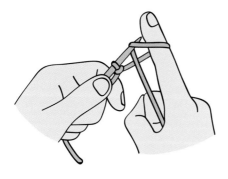

4. Repeat steps 2 and 3.

Backward-Loop Cast On

Also called Simple Cast On, Single Cast On, Half-Hitch Cast On, Twisted-Loop Cast On, Knit-Loop Cast On, Thread-Over-the-Thumb Cast On, Right-Slanting-Loop Cast On

This is the reverse of the loop cast on (page 13), with the stitches slanting in the opposite direction. It has the same properties as the previous technique, including the same advantages and disadvantages.

Backward-loop cast on

1. Hold the needle in the right hand and the yarn taut between both hands, with the ball on the left and the tail in the right fingers. (You can also use a slipknot.) *Swing the left thumb behind and under the strand, and then forward and up to create a loop around the thumb.

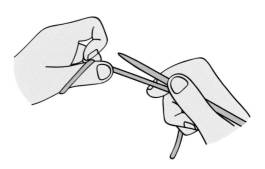

2. Insert the needle into the loop as if to knit.

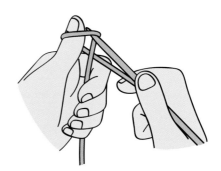

3. Release the loop on the thumb and pull the yarn to tighten the stitch. Repeat from *.

On the first row, slip the first stitch, and then knit the remaining stitches through the back loop. For a firmer edge, knit the first row normally, through the front of the loops. This will twist the stitches.

Alternate-Loop Cast On

This technique alternates the loop and backward-loop cast ons (pages 13 and 14). It makes a series of half-hitch knots, creating horizontal bars along the edge.

Alternate-loop cast on

1. Make a slipknot about 5" from the end of the strand and place it on the needle. Hold the needle in the right hand and hold the strand taut in the left fingers. *Swing the left index finger in front of the strand, under it, and up, catching the strand on the finger.

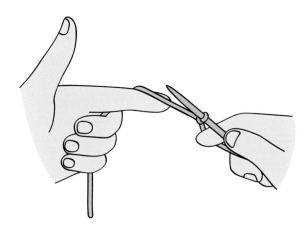

2. Crook the finger and move it forward toward the thumb to create a loop on the finger. Insert the needle into the loop from right to left.

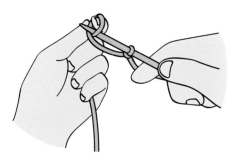

3. Remove the finger from the loop and pull the yarn to tighten the stitch.

4. Swing the left thumb behind and under the strand, and then forward and up to create a loop around the thumb.

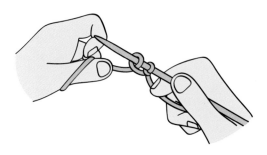

5. Insert the needle into the thumb loop as if to knit.

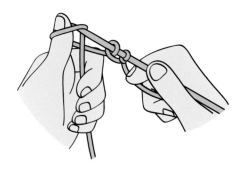

6. Release the loop on the thumb and pull the tail to tighten the stitch. Repeat from *.

Twisted-Loop Cast On

Also called Elastic Cast On, Twisted Simple Cast On

When you're knitting neckbands or sock cuffs that need to be both stretchy and durable, this is a dependable option. And since it's difficult to make this too tight, it's great for beginners. The small eyelets created along the cast-on edge pair nicely with fringe added as a decorative element.

Twisted-loop cast on

1. With the needle in the left hand, hold the yarn taut between both hands with the tail on the left and the ball on the right.

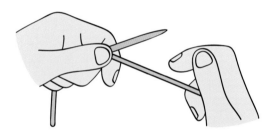

2. Swing the right thumb and index finger over, behind, and under the yarn, and then up to wrap the strand around both the thumb and the finger.

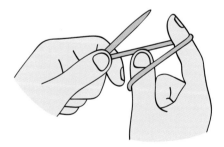

3. Turn the index finger away from you, crook it, and bring it down and forward to the right of the strand around the thumb.

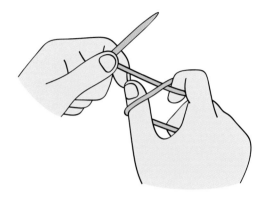

4. Rotate the right hand, swing the finger up, and straighten it to create a twisted loop on the finger.

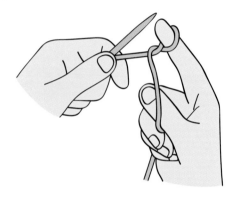

5. Insert the needle into the loop from left to right. Remove the finger and pull the yarn to tighten the stitch.

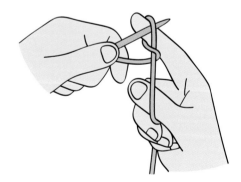

6. Repeat steps 2–5.

Twisted-Loop Cast On: Czech Variation

Charlene Schurch learned this Czech variation from her mother. It differs from the others by having the bumps on the right side and the slanted strands on the back; also, the strands slant from right to left rather than left to right.

Twisted-loop cast on: Czech variation

1. Make a slipknot about 5" from the end of the yarn and place it on the needle. *Holding the needle in the right hand, bring the yarn between the left pinky and fourth finger from back to front, between the index finger and thumb from front to back, and around the thumb to the front. Next bring the yarn between the index and middle fingers from front to back, around the middle finger, and back to the front between the middle and fourth fingers.

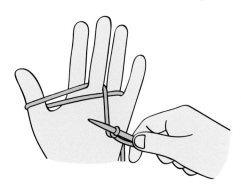

2. Insert the needle under the crossed strands between the thumb and fingers.

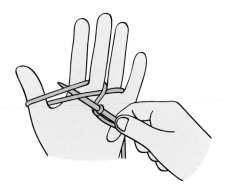

3. Bring the needle up and to the right to catch the strand between the thumb and middle finger.

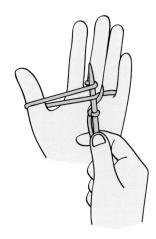

4. Pull the strand down and to the right under the strand between the pinky and thumb and up between the two strands around the middle finger. Remove the loops around the thumb and middle finger and pull the yarn to tighten the stitch. Repeat from *.

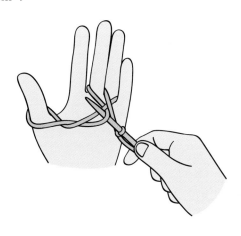

Twisted-Loop Cast On: Double-Twist Variation

This variation creates a firmer edge with knots along it. If your yarn is loosely spun or plied, this method can make it challenging to keep the yarn intact—proceed with great care.

Twisted-loop cast on: double-twist variation

Follow the directions for the twisted-loop cast on (page 16), but in step 4 rotate the right finger twice. Be sure to slide the new stitch snugly against the adjacent stitch before tightening it.

Long-Tail Cast Ons

The long-tail cast ons are probably the most commonly used. All these methods start by leaving a long tail in the yarn; hence the name. After you measure off a length of yarn, you make a slipknot and then work the cast on using both the working end of the yarn and the tail.

This is a large, diverse group of cast ons that produce neat, even edges. Most are firm yet elastic and are good all-around choices for the majority of projects.

The twisted long-tail cast ons produce particularly stretchy edges, perfect for sock cuffs and hats.

Determining Tail Length

The trickiest part of these cast ons is figuring out how long the tail should be. It's extremely frustrating to be halfway through casting on, only to discover that the tail is insufficient. Leaving too much of a tail is less of a problem, as you can use the leftover segment later to sew a seam.

One way to calculate tail length is to allow 1" per stitch. This method is not terribly accurate, since larger needles and thicker yarn will require more than 1" for each stitch while smaller needles and thinner yarn will require less, but it does give you a useful starting point. Another method is to wrap the yarn around the needle once for every stitch. Holding the yarn at the last wrap, pull out the needle and add a few extra inches before making the slipknot. A third way, which is probably the most reliable, calls for the tail to be three times the width of the piece to be cast on. For example, if your piece will be 10" wide, you'll need a tail about 30" long.

If you think you do not have enough tail to finish casting on, you can switch the tail with the working yarn. When making a stitch, more of the tail yarn is used than the working yarn; switching the two can make the tail yarn last longer. The switching will create a small twist along the bottom edge, but it will not be noticeable.

To avoid having to estimate the length of the tail altogether, you can use two balls of yarn. Tie the two ends together in a slipknot and place it on the needle. Then use one strand as the working yarn and the other as the tail. When counting the cast-on stitches, do not count the slipknot. After casting on, cut the tail strand, leaving a tail at least 5" long. Work the first row, stopping just before the slipknot. Undo the slipknot and continue knitting.

Basic Long-Tail Cast On

Also called Continental Cast On, German Cast On, Double Cast On, Finger Cast On, Y Cast On, Slingshot Cast On, Two-Strand Cast On, One-Needle Cast On, Single-Needle Cast On, Twisted Cast On, Half-Hitch Cast On, Two-Tail Cast On

The long-tail cast on creates a neat and even edge. Because it is firm yet elastic, it wears well and is a useful all-purpose cast on for most types of projects. When used with stockinette stitch, the edge will curl. The two sides of the edge are different, and you can choose either one for your right side.

This is an excellent technique to become familiar with, because it provides the basis for many other cast ons and bind offs. Consider pairing it with the sewn bind off (page 144), stem-stitch bind off (page 146), or standard bind off (page 114).

Long-tail cast on, bump side

Long-tail cast on, slanted strands side

Basic Long-Tail Cast On: Continental Method

1. Leaving a long tail, make a slipknot and place it on the needle. Hold the needle in the right hand with both strands in the left fingers. Insert the left thumb and index finger between the strands and spread them apart.

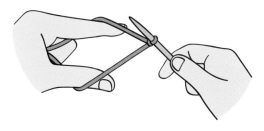

2. Turn the thumb and index finger up to wrap the tail around the thumb and the working strand around the finger. Hold both ends in the remaining fingers of the left hand.

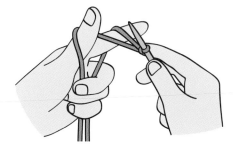

3. Insert the needle into the thumb loop as if to knit.

4. Catch the front finger strand with the needle from the right.

5. Pull the strand back down through the thumb loop.

6. Remove the thumb from the loop, insert the thumb between the strands, and pull the tail toward you to tighten the stitch. Swing the thumb up to create a new thumb loop.

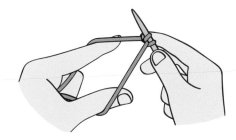

7. Repeat steps 3–6.

Basic Long-Tail Cast On: Continental Method Variation

Also called Russian Cast On

    Casting on over two needles guarantees the edge will not be tight, but the stitches of the bottom row are elongated, making the edge slightly more open.

Long-tail cast on: continental method variation

1. Leaving a long tail, wrap the yarn around the left thumb and index finger, with the tail on the left and the working yarn on the right. Hold both ends in the remaining fingers of the left hand.

2. Holding two needles together, place them under the strand between the thumb and the index finger. Lift the needles slightly against the strand and place the right index finger on top of the strand to hold it in place. Then follow steps 3–6 on page 19, casting on over the two needles.

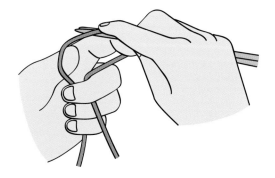

    When all the stitches have been cast on, remove one needle and begin your project.

Basic Long-Tail Cast On: English Method

Also called Thumb Cast On, Right-Finger Half-Hitch Cast On, Knit Half-Hitch Cast On

1. Leaving a long tail, make a slipknot and place it on the needle. Hold the needle in the right hand with the ball on the right. Holding the tail in the left fingers, *swing the left thumb over, behind, and under the tail, and then up to wrap the strand around the thumb.

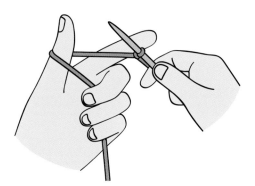

2. Insert the needle into the loop as if to knit.

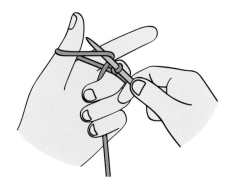

3. Wrap the working strand around the needle. Pull the strand through the thumb loop. Remove the thumb from the loop and pull the tail to tighten the stitch. Repeat from *.

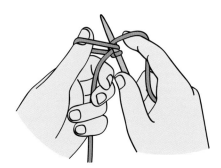

Basic Long-Tail Cast On: English Method Variation

Also called Italian Cast On

1. Leaving a long tail, make a slipknot and place it on the needle. Hold the needle in the right hand with the ball on the right. *Holding the tail taut in the left fingers, swing the left thumb and index finger over, behind, and under the strand, and then up to wrap the yarn around both the thumb and the finger.

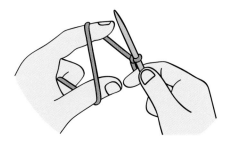

2. Insert the needle into the finger loop as if to knit.

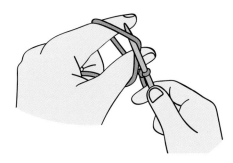

3. With the right hand, wrap the working yarn around the needle as if to knit.

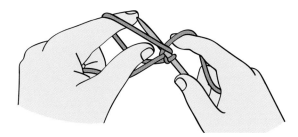

4. Lift the loop on the left index finger up and over the tip of the needle. Remove the index finger and pull the tail to tighten the stitch. Repeat from *.

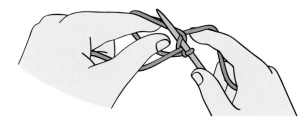

Double Long-Tail Cast On

Also called Multi-Strand Cast On

The use of two strands creates an edge that offers durability but not great elasticity. It's also thicker than most cast-on edges. Some versions double only the thumb strand, keeping the index finger or wrapping strand single to create a slightly thinner edge.

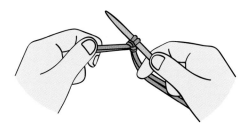

Double long-tail cast on

1. With two strands of yarn together, leave a long tail, make a slipknot, and place it on the needle.

2. Cast on using either long-tail method with double strands on both the thumb and the index finger. The cast-on stitches will be two strands. Drop one strand (which you'll weave in later) and begin your project, working each pair of strands as one stitch.

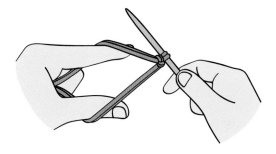

Double Long-Tail Cast On: Two-Strand Variation

Also called Multi-Strand Cast On

Frequently used on traditional fishermen's ganseys, this cast on creates a very firm, durable edge for ribbing. It requires needles three to four sizes smaller than the project needles.

Double long-tail cast on: two-strand variation

1. With two strands of yarn together, leave a long tail, make a slipknot, and place it on the smaller needle. Cast on with either the continental or English method of the long-tail cast on (pages 19 and 20), using the double strands on both the thumb and index finger, or to wrap.
2. With the smaller needles, work four to six rows with two strands. Then drop one strand and change to the larger project needles to continue knitting.

Double Long-Tail Cast On: Thumb Variation

Also called Double Two-Strand Cast On

This variation doubles only the thumb strand. Tightening up the stitches takes a bit of practice; the same edge can be achieved more easily with the three-strand variation (at right).

Double long-tail cast on: thumb variation

1. Leaving a slightly longer tail than usual, make a slipknot and place it on the needle. Hold the needle in the right hand with the working strand on the right and the tail on the left. Wrap the tail around the thumb twice.

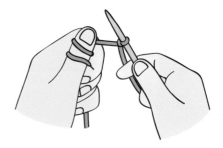

2. Insert the needle into the double loop as if to knit and follow the steps for the long-tail cast on: English method (page 20).

Double Long-Tail Cast On: Three-Strand Variation

This variation uses three strands, but only the thumb strand is doubled.

1. Measure out a tail twice as long as usual, and then double the yarn back on itself. Make a slipknot several inches from the end of the yarn and place it on the needle.

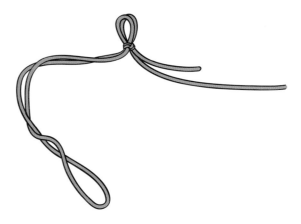

2. Holding the short end in the right fingers, cast on using the long-tail cast on: continental method (page 19) with the double strand around the thumb and the single strand around the index finger.

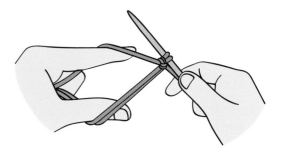

Triple Long-Tail Cast On

This Scandinavian variation of the double long-tail cast on (page 21) uses three strands around the thumb, resulting in an edge that is thick and quite durable.

Triple long-tail cast on

1. Leaving a tail three times longer than usual, make a slipknot and place it on the needle. Loop the long tail over the needle so that it makes three equal strands.

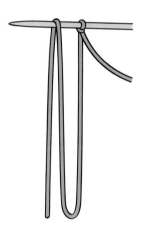

2. Using the three strands together as the thumb strand, cast on using either the continental or the English method of the long-tail cast on (pages 19 and 20). Count the slipknot and the stitch next to it as one stitch.

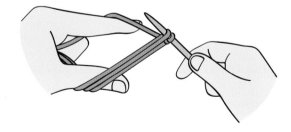

Triple Long-Tail Cast On Variation

Here is another Scandinavian version that creates a thick, open edge.

Triple long-tail cast on variation

1. Measure out a tail about three times longer than usual and loop the yarn so that it makes three equal strands.

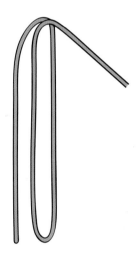

2. Insert the needle into the loop at the top of the three strands.

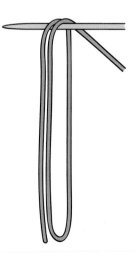

3. Holding the strands in place on the needle with the right index finger, wrap the three strands together around the thumb and the single strand attached to the ball over the index finger.

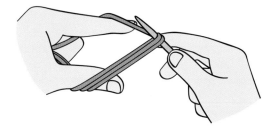

4. Cast on the first stitch using the long-tail cast on: continental method (page 19), but do not remove the thumb from the loop.

5. Cast on a second stitch by swinging the needle over the front thumb triple strand, down in front of the back triple strand, and under it.

6. Swing the needle up to catch the front finger strand with the needle from the right.

7. Pull the strand back through the thumb loop, remove the thumb from the loop, and pull the tail to tighten the stitch. Insert the thumb between the thumb and finger strands and swing the thumb up to create a new thumb loop.

Repeat steps 4–7. You will be casting on two stitches with each repeat.

Purl the first row (wrong side), and then knit the right side and establish your pattern.

Combined Long-Tail Cast On

Also called Combined Two-Strand Cast On, Double-Start Cast On, Estonian Cast On, Latvian Cast On, Double-Crossed Cast On

This variation of the long-tail cast on (page 18) alternates the direction of wrapping the yarn around the thumb. You can use it with either the continental or the English method. The stitches are grouped in pairs on the needle, with the purl bar creating a decorative effect.

You'll cast on an uneven number of stitches. If you need an even number, stop with step 4 or increase or decrease a stitch when you start your project.

Combined long-tail cast on

1. Leaving a long tail, make a slipknot and place it on the needle. Hold the needle in the right hand with both strands in the left fingers. Insert the left thumb

and index finger between the strands and spread them apart. Hold both ends in the remaining fingers of the left hand.

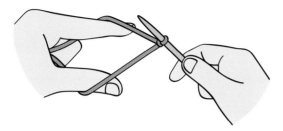

2. Wrap the tail around the thumb clockwise, and insert the needle into the thumb loop as if to knit.

3. Catch the finger strand with the needle from the right.

4. Pull the strand down through the thumb loop, remove the thumb from the loop, insert the thumb between the strands, and pull the tail toward you to tighten the stitch.

5. Wrap the tail around the thumb counterclockwise.

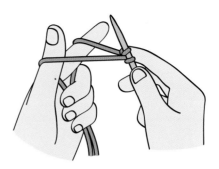

6. Insert the needle between the two thumb strands and under the back thumb strand.

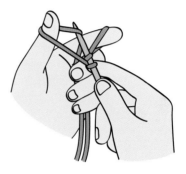

7. Swing the needle to the right to catch the front index-finger strand from the right.

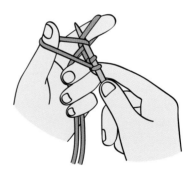

8. Pull the strand back through the thumb loop, remove the thumb from the loop, and pull the tail to tighten the stitch.

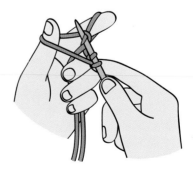

9. Repeat steps 2–8. The first row is the wrong side if working flat.

Combined Long-Tail Cast On: Italian Variation

1. Leaving a long tail, make a slipknot and place it on the needle. Hold the needle in the right hand with the ball on the right. *Holding the tail taut in the left fingers, swing the left thumb and index finger over, behind, and under the strand, and then up to wrap the yarn around both the thumb and the finger.

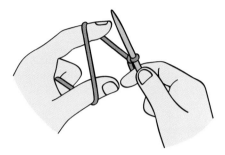

2. Insert the needle into the finger loop as if to knit.

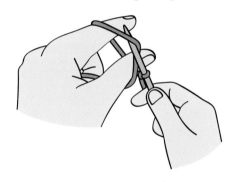

3. With the right hand, wrap the working yarn around the needle as if to knit.

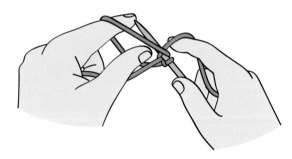

4. Bring the loop on the left index finger up and over the tip of the needle, remove the index finger, and pull the tail to tighten the stitch.

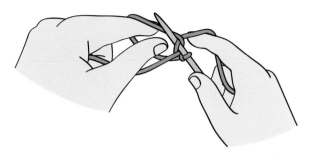

5. Holding the tail taut, swing the left index finger forward over the strand.

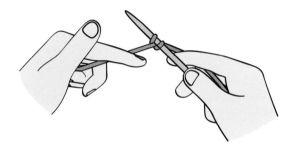

6. Bring the finger down in front of the strand, under it, and up to wrap it over the finger. Crook the finger and rotate it to the left, making a loop on the finger.

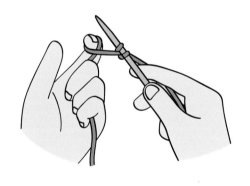

7. Insert the needle into the loop as if to knit.

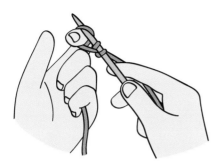

8. Wrap the working yarn around the needle as if to knit.

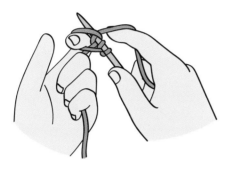

9. Lift the finger loop over and off the needle, remove the finger from the loop, and pull the tail to tighten the stitch.
10. Repeat from *. The first row is the wrong side if working flat.

Combined Long-Tail Cast On: Thick Variation

The double strand around the thumb creates a thick, decorative edge. You cast on an even number of stitches.

Combined long-tail cast on: thick variation

1. Leaving a tail twice as long as usual, double the yarn back on itself, make a slipknot with both strands together about 5" from the end of the yarn, and place the knot on the right needle.

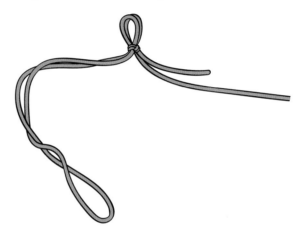

2. Holding the short end in the right fingers, follow steps 1–8 of the combined long-tail cast on (page 24) with the double strand around the thumb and the single strand around the index finger.

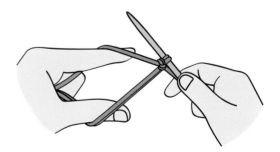

Simplified Cast On

The reverse of the long-tail cast on (page 18), this method results in slanting strands on the right side. They also slant in the opposite direction. In all other respects, it's the same as the long-tail cast on. Consider the simplified cast on when you want the purl bumps on the right side.

Simplified cast on

Simplified Cast On: Continental Method

1. Leaving a long tail, make a slipknot and place it on the needle. Hold the needle in the right hand with both strands in the left fingers. Insert the left index finger between the strands and bring it up to wrap the strand around the finger. *Swing the thumb counterclockwise around the tail strand to create a loop around the thumb.

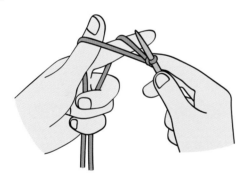

2. Insert the needle between the thumb strands and under the back thumb strand.

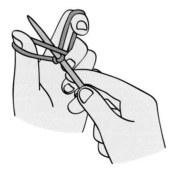

3. Catch the front finger strand from the right.

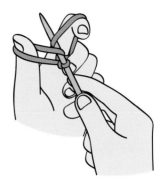

4. Pull the strand back through the thumb loop, remove the thumb from the loop, insert the thumb between the strands, and spread them apart to tighten the stitch. Repeat from *.

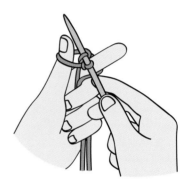

Simplified Cast On: English Method

1. Leaving a long tail, make a slipknot and place it on the needle. Hold the needle in the right hand with the ball on the right. *Holding the tail taut in the left fingers, bring the left index finger forward over the tail, then down and under it, behind, and up to wrap the yarn around the finger.

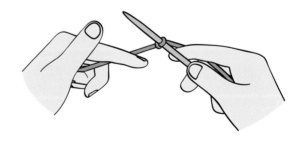

2. Crook the finger so that the tip points to the left, creating a loop on the finger. Insert the needle into the loop as if to knit.

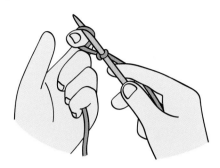

3. Wrap the working yarn around the needle, pull the yarn back through the loop, remove the left finger from the loop, and pull the tail to tighten the stitch. Repeat from *.

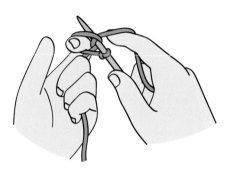

Left-Handed Cast On

This cast on is the reverse of the long-tail cast on: continental method (page 19), producing an edge that is the mirror image. The slanted strands along the edge lean to the left rather than the right.

Left-handed cast on

1. Leaving a long tail, make a slipknot and place it on the needle. Hold the needle in the left hand and hold both strands in the right fingers. Insert the right thumb and index finger between the strands, spread them apart, and turn them up to wrap the tail around the thumb and the working strand around the index finger. Hold both ends in the right fingers.

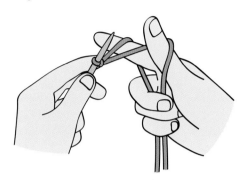

2. Insert the needle into the thumb loop as if to knit.

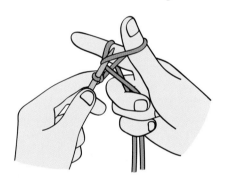

3. Catch the front finger strand with the needle from the left and above, and pull it back down through the thumb loop. Remove the thumb from the loop, insert the thumb between the strands, and pull the tail to tighten the stitch. Swing the thumb up to create a new loop.

4. Repeat steps 2 and 3.

Two-Needle Cast On

This cast-on edge mirrors the edge of the long-tail cast on (page 18), with the stitches slanting in the opposite direction.

Two-needle cast on

1. Leaving a long tail, make a slipknot and place it on the needle. Hold the needle in the left hand. *Bring the tail behind the working yarn and wrap it over the needle from back to front.

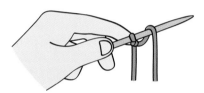

2. Bring the working yarn in front of the tail and wrap it over the needle from back to front.

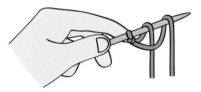

3. Hold the two strands taut with the left thumb and index finger. With a second needle, lift the second stitch in from the tip of the needle over the stitch closest to the needle tip and off the needle. Pull the tail to tighten the stitch. Repeat from *.

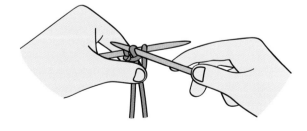

Cast On with One Needle

This is the reverse of the long-tail cast on (page 18), with the slanting strands on the opposite side. This is a good choice for circular knitting when you want the purl bumps on the right side.

Cast on with one needle

1. Leaving a long tail, make a slipknot and place it on the needle. Hold the needle in the right hand with the working yarn in the right fingers. *Swing the right index finger over, behind, and under the working yarn, and then up to wrap the strand over the finger.

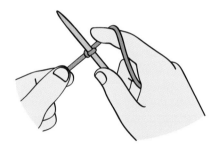

2. Rotate the right hand to the left to create a loop on the finger, and slip the loop onto the needle, but keep the finger in the loop.

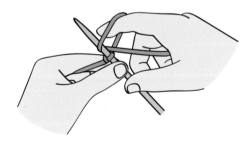

3. With the left hand, wrap the tail over the needle from front to back.

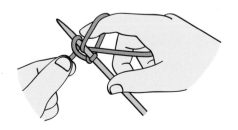

4. Bring the loop on the index finger down over the needle tip, and then remove the finger and pull the working end to tighten the stitch. Repeat from *.

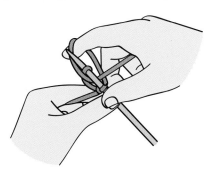

Purled Half-Hitch Cast On

This method is the reverse of the long-tail cast on (page 18), with the slanting strands on the opposite side and angled in the opposite direction. It is good for circular knitting when you want the purl bumps on the right side.

Purled half-hitch cast on

1. Leaving a long tail, make a slipknot and place it on the needle. Hold the needle in the right hand with both strands in the left fingers. Insert the left thumb and index finger between the strands, spread them apart, and turn them up to wrap the tail around the thumb and the working yarn around the index finger. Hold both ends in the fingers of the left hand.

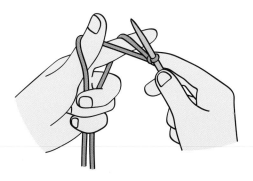

2. Swing the needle to the right and behind the back finger strand, and then forward into the finger loop.

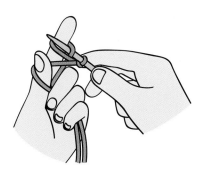

3. Bring the needle forward over the front finger strand, and then under the back thumb strand and up to catch it.

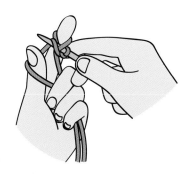

4. Pull the strand back through the finger loop, remove the finger from the loop, and insert it between the strands. Pull the working strand away from you to tighten the stitch.

5. Repeat steps 2–4.

Long-Tail Cast On in Pattern

This variation of the long-tail cast on (page 18) allows you to make knit and purl stitches so that the edge is the same as your pattern stitch. It uses the long-tail cast on: English method. If you prefer the long-tail cast on: continental method, use the K1, P1 rib cast on (at right) for the same effect.

Long-tail cast on in pattern

1. Leaving a long tail, make a slipknot and place it on the needle. This is a knit stitch. Hold the needle in the right hand with the ball on the right and the tail in the left fingers. For a knit stitch, *swing the left thumb over, behind, and under the tail, and then up to wrap the strand around the thumb.

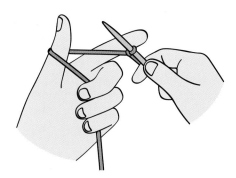

2. Insert the needle into the thumb loop as if to knit.

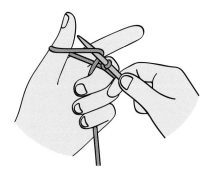

3. Wrap the working yarn around the needle as if to knit, pull the strand through the thumb loop, remove the thumb from the loop, and pull the tail to tighten the stitch.

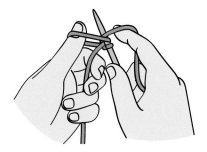

4. For a purl stitch, bring the yarn to the front and wrap the tail strand around the thumb as in step 1. Insert the needle under the front thumb strand from right to left.

   Wrap the yarn around the needle as if to purl, and pull the yarn back through the thumb loop. Remove the thumb and tighten the stitch.

5. Repeat from *, working knit and purl stitches according to your pattern stitch. Drop the slipknot if you don't want two knit stitches together at the beginning of the row.

K1, P1 Rib Cast On

Also called K+P Cast On, 1 x 1 Rib Cast On, Long-Tail Cast On in Pattern

   Combining the purled half-hitch cast on (page 31) with the long-tail cast on (page 18), this method works well for double knitting and can be performed with two colors.

K1, P1 rib cast on

1. Leaving a long tail, make a slipknot and place it on the needle. This is the knit stitch. Insert the left thumb and index finger between the strands, spread them apart, and turn them up to wrap the tail around the thumb and the working strand around the index finger.

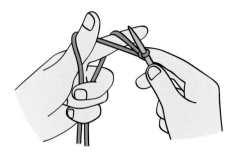

2. Swing the needle to the right and behind the back index-finger strand, and then forward into the finger loop.

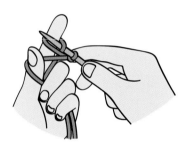

3. Bring the needle forward over the front index-finger strand, and then under the back thumb strand and up to catch it.

4. Pull the strand back through the finger loop. Remove the finger from the loop, insert it between the two strands of yarn, and move it away from you to tighten the stitch. This is the purl stitch.

5. Cast on one stitch using the long-tail cast on: continental method (page 19). Insert the needle into the thumb loop as if to knit.

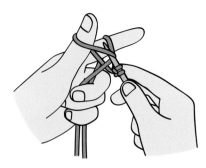

6. Catch the finger strand with the needle from the right.

7. Pull the strand down through the thumb loop, and remove the thumb from the loop. Insert the thumb between the strands, pull the tail toward you to tighten the stitch, and swing the thumb up to create a new thumb loop.

8. Repeat steps 2–7, alternating a knit stitch and a purl stitch, and end with step 4. As you learn this cast on, you may find it helpful to place the right index finger on top of each new stitch to keep it in position before releasing the finger loop.

K1, P1 Rib Cast On: K2, P2 Variation

Also called K+P Cast On Variation; K2, P2 Rib Cast On
Work as for K1, P1 rib cast on (page 32), but alternate making two knit stitches and two purl stitches.

German Twisted Cast On

Also called Twisted German Cast On, Twisted Cast On, Elastic Long-Tail Cast On, Elastic Cast On, Old Norwegian Cast On, Old Norwegian Sock Cast On, English Cast On, Twisted Half-Hitch Cast On, Twisted-Loop Cast On

Creating an edge that is both elastic and firm, the German twisted cast on is useful for a wide range of projects, but particularly suitable for corrugated ribbing as it helps prevent the lower edge from curling.

German twisted cast on

German Twisted Cast On: Continental Method

1. Leaving a long tail, make a slipknot and place it on the needle. Hold the needle in the right hand with both strands in the left fingers. *Insert the left thumb and index finger between the strands, spread them apart, and turn them up to wrap the tail around the thumb and the working yarn around the index finger. Hold both ends with the remaining fingers of the left hand.

2. Insert the needle under both thumb strands.

3. Bring the needle up, over the back thumb strand and down into the thumb loop, and then forward, under, and up over the front thumb strand.

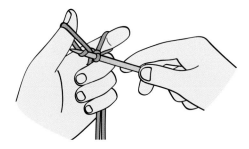

4. Swing the needle back and over the near index-finger strand.

5. Catch the index-finger strand and pull it forward. At the same time, bend the left thumb down and away from you to open up the thumb loop.

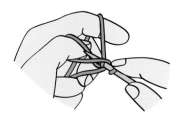

6. Bring the needle down through the thumb loop, and then forward and up. Remove the thumb from the loop, insert it between the strands, and pull both tails to tighten the stitch. Repeat from *.

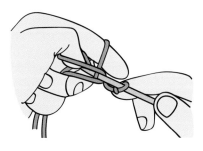

CAST ONS

German Twisted Cast On: Continental Method Variation

This knotless Scandinavian variation is often executed with two colors.

Hold two strands of yarn together taut in both hands, with the balls on the left. With the needle in the right hand, swing it forward, under the strands, and up to wrap the strands around the needle. Then cast on using the German twisted cast on: continental method opposite.

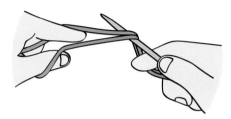

German Twisted Cast On: English Method

Also called Twisted Right-Finger Half-Hitch Cast On

1. Leaving a long tail, make a slipknot and place it on the needle. *Holding the tail in the left fingers, swing the left thumb over, behind, and under the tail, and then up to wrap the tail around the thumb.

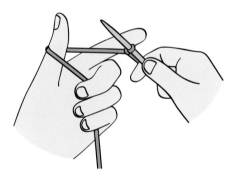

2. Insert the needle under both thumb strands.

3. Bring the needle up and over the back thumb strand and down into the thumb loop.

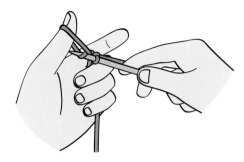

4. Swing the needle forward, up, and to the right of the thumb, and wrap the working yarn around the needle as if to knit.

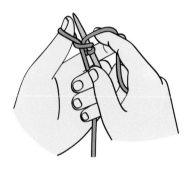

5. Bend the left thumb down and away from you to open the thumb loop, and bring the needle down through the thumb loop, forward, and up.

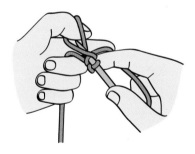

6. Release the thumb loop and pull both ends to tighten the stitch. Repeat from *.

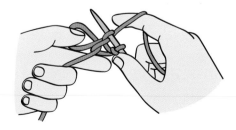

Twisted Italian Cast On

Also called Twisted-Loop Cast On

This cast on produces the same edge as the German twisted cast on (page 34), with the same characteristics.

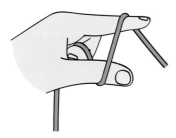

Twisted Italian cast on

1. Leaving a long tail, hold the yarn taut between both hands with the ball on the right and the tail on the left. *Swing the left thumb and index finger over, behind, and under the yarn, and then up to wrap the yarn around both the thumb and the finger.

2. With the right hand, insert the needle between the left thumb and index finger to the left of the yarn, move the needle to the right under the back finger strand, catch the strand, and bring it forward.

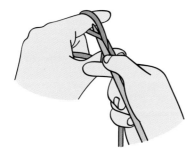

3. Bring the needle up and to the right to create a figure eight, with loops on the needle and index finger.

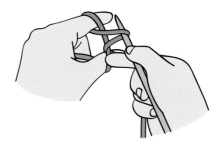

4. With the right index finger, wrap the working yarn around the needle as if to knit.

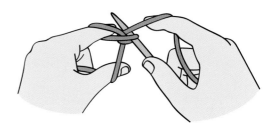

5. Crook the left index finger and rotate it upward to open up the loop. Pull the loop up and over the needle tip, remove the index finger from the loop, and pull the left thumb toward you to tighten stitch. Repeat from *.

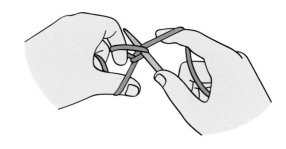

English Cast On

Also called Maine Cast On

Here is another variation of the German twisted cast on (page 34), producing the same edge and featuring the same characteristics.

English cast on

1. Leaving a long tail, hold the yarn taut in both hands with the ball on the right and the tail on the left. *Swing the left thumb over, behind, and under the strand, and then up to wrap the strand around the thumb.

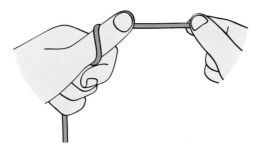

2. Bring the left index finger forward over the strand, and crook the finger to catch the strand.

3. Move the finger to the left to position it above the thumb.

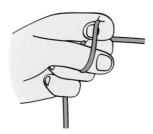

4. Straighten the finger so that it points to the right, creating a loop on the finger.

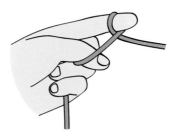

5. Insert the needle into the finger loop as if to knit, wrap the working yarn around the needle as if to knit, and pull the strand through the loop. Remove the finger from the loop and pull the tail to tighten the stitch. Repeat from *.

Twisted Cast On

This Scandinavian cast on is used in two-strand knitting and can be performed in one or two steps. The one-step version is the same as the German twisted cast on (page 34). The two-step version shown here is not a long-tail cast on but is included here because of its close relationship to the German twisted cast on.

With a firm but elastic edge, this cast on lends itself well to the use of different colors for a variety of decorative effects. You can cast on in one color and knit the first row with another; or you could use two different-colored strands and alternate casting on, one stitch of one, one of the other; or do the same with three different colors.

This cast on requires using needles one size larger than the project needles. Once the stitches are cast on, switch to the smaller project needles.

Twisted cast on

1. Hold the strand taut in both hands with the ball on the left. With the needle in the right hand, swing it forward over the strand, under it, and up to wrap the yarn around the needle. (You can also use a slipknot.) *Swing the thumb over, behind, and under the strand, and then up to wrap the strand around the thumb.

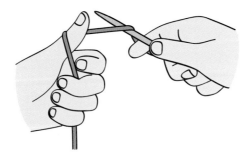

2. Insert the needle under both thumb strands.

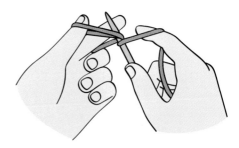

3. Swing the needle up over the back thumb strand to catch it and pull it forward under the front thumb strand.

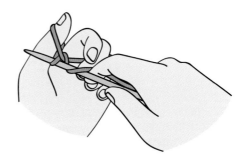

4. Remove the thumb from the loop and pull the strand to tighten the stitch.

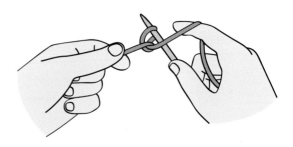

5. Repeat from *. Knit the first row through the front loops of the stitches.

Double-Twist Cast On

This cast on is used in Scandinavian two-strand knitting. It is a variation of the German twisted cast on (page 34) and creates an elastic, decorative edge. You can also use two or three different colored yarns to create a very vibrant edge.

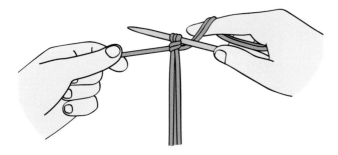

Double-twist cast on

1. Make a slipknot with three strands of yarn together about 5" from their ends and place the knot on the right needle. Hold strand 1 in the left hand and strands 2 and 3 in the right hand.

2. Swing the left thumb over, behind, and under strand 1, and then up to create a loop on the thumb. Insert the needle under both thumb strands.

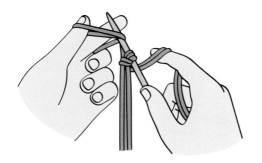

3. Bring the needle up and over the back thumb strand, and then forward, down through the thumb loop, and up.

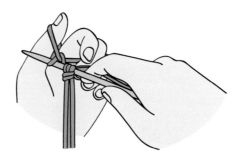

4. Wrap strand 2 around the needle as if to knit.

5. Bring the needle back down through the thumb loop, forward, and up, release the thumb loop, and pull both ends to tighten the stitch.

Repeat steps 2–5, wrapping with strand 3. Continue wrapping alternating strands 2 and 3. Drop the slipknot from the needle on the first row.

Austrian Cast On

Like the German twisted cast on (page 34), this is another twisted cast on that creates an elastic edge less likely to curl. It's difficult to master, however, since the strands tend to knot up. Keep everything open as you gently pull both strands evenly, and do the final tightening only when the strands are in place. Practicing on a smooth, slippery yarn may help you learn to control the tension.

Austrian cast on

1. Leaving a long tail, make a slipknot and place it on the needle. Hold the needle in the right hand with both strands in the left fingers. Insert the left thumb and index finger between the strands, spread them apart, and turn them up to wrap the tail around the thumb and the working yarn around the index finger.

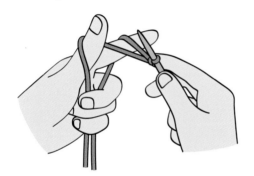

2. Insert the needle into the thumb loop as if to knit.

3. Swing the needle over the back thumb strand and both finger strands, down behind the back finger strand, under the strand, and up to catch it.

4. Bring the needle forward over the front finger strand, through the thumb loop, and up. Remove the thumb and finger from the loops, insert them between the two strands, and spread them apart to tighten the stitch.

5. Repeat steps 2–4.

Thumb Cast On

Also called Twisted Right-Finger Half-Hitch Cast On

Although the thumb cast on is reputed to come from the Shetland Islands, there are those who disagree. Rhoda Hughson of the Unst Heritage Centre consulted with numerous knitters there, and they report that while the thumb cast on is indeed used in that area, it is not thought to be particularly associated with Shetland. Regardless of its heritage, this technique produces an edge similar to that of the German twisted cast on (page 34) and is well suited for the garter stitch, as the edge mimics the garter stitch ridge.

Thumb cast on, right side

Thumb cast on, wrong side

1. Leaving a long tail, make a slipknot and place it on the needle. *Holding the tail in the left fingers, swing the left thumb counterclockwise around the tail twice, creating a cross on the front of the thumb.

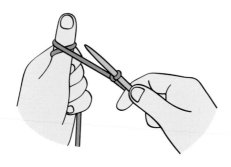

2. Insert the needle into the right side of the thumb loop as if to knit, and wrap the working yarn around the needle as if to knit.

3. Pull the yarn through the thumb loop and then out between the two right arms of the cross. Remove the thumb from the loop, and pull the tail to tighten the stitches. Repeat from *.

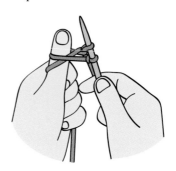

Channel Island Cast On

Also called Knotted Cast On

This versatile cast on creates a strong, stretchy edge distinguished by a row of decorative beads. While popular in the making of traditional ganseys, it is also a fun, functional cast on for socks knit from the cuff down. It was originally used with garter stitch, but it also works well with K1, P1 rib. Note that you'll be making two stitches at a time.

Channel Island cast on in garter stitch

Channel Island cast on in K1, P1 rib

Channel Island Cast On: Continental Method

1. Leaving a long tail, bring the end up to the starting point to create a long double strand.

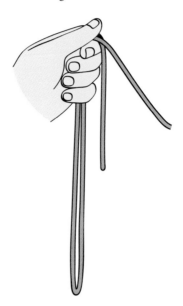

2. Wrap the left thumb counterclockwise twice around the double strand. The loop will hang on the left. Hold the tail end in the left fingers for the first few stitches to keep it from getting lost.

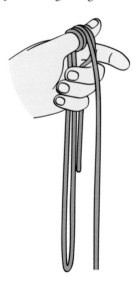

CAST ONS

3. Drape the single strand attached to the ball over the left index finger as for the long-tail cast on (page 18). Place the needle under the single strand stretching between the thumb and index finger. Bring the needle up, forward, and to the left to catch the strand on the needle, creating a yarn over.

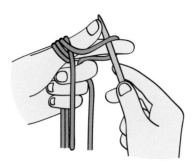

4. Insert the needle into the thumb loop under all four strands as if to knit.

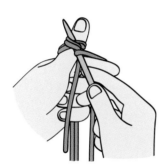

5. Catch the front finger strand from the right and pull it back through the thumb loop, remove the thumb from the loop, insert it between the strands, and pull it toward you to tighten the stitch. You may need to tug the double strand gently at the end to produce the knot/stitch.

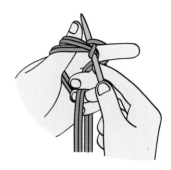

6. Wrap the double strand counterclockwise twice around the thumb, and swing the needle to the right, over, behind, and under the near index-finger strand to create a yarn over.

Repeat steps 5 and 6, ending with step 6. When using this cast on with K1, P1 ribbing in the round, start the first row with K1. You'll knit the knots and purl the yarn overs. If you purl the knot, the bead will be less pronounced. If you are working flat, start the first row (wrong side) with P1. You'll purl the knots and knit the yarn overs.

Channel Island Cast On: English Method

1. Leaving a long tail, bring the end of the yarn up to the starting point to create a long double strand in your left fingers.

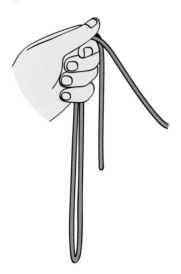

2. Wrap the double strand of yarn counterclockwise twice around the thumb. Hold the loop and the tail end in the left fingers. After the first few stitches, you can drop the tail.

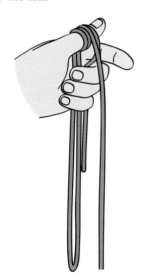

3. With the needle in the right hand, swing it under the strand, up, and over to catch the strand on the needle, creating a yarn over.

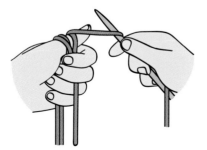

4. Insert the needle into the thumb loop under all four thumb strands as if to knit.

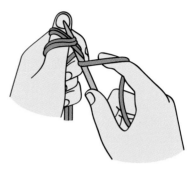

5. Wrap the working yarn around the needle as if to knit and pull it through the thumb loop, remove the thumb from the loop, and pull the double strand to tighten the stitch. You may need to tug the double strand gently at the end to produce the knot/stitch.

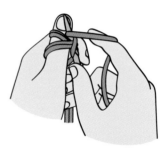

6. Rotate the thumb counterclockwise twice around the double strand. Bring the working yarn to the front to create a yarn over.

7. Repeat steps 4–6, ending with step 5.

When using this cast on with K1, P1 ribbing in the round, start the first row with K1. You'll knit the knots and purl the yarn overs. If you purl the knot, the bead will be less pronounced. If you are working flat, start the first row (wrong side) with P1. You'll purl the knots and knit the yarn overs.

Knotted Cast On

Also called Guernsey Cast On

This durable but flexible edge is decorated with little knots. It has a tendency to widen, especially if worked too loosely, so it's not well suited for ribbing. Using needles three to four sizes smaller than the project needles will help to keep the edge's widening ways under control. This cast on is based on the long-tail cast on (page 18), with variations using the backward-loop cast on (page 14) and the knit cast on (page 48).

Knotted cast on

1. Leaving a tail slightly longer than usual, make a slipknot and place it on the needle. Hold the needle in the right hand with the ball on the right. Holding the tail in the left fingers, cast on two stitches using the long-tail cast on: English method (page 20) as follows: *swing the left thumb over, behind, and under the tail, and then up to wrap the strand around the thumb.

2. Insert the needle into the thumb loop as if to knit.

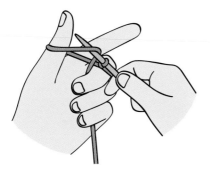

3. Wrap the working yarn around the needle as if to knit. Pull the strand through the thumb loop, remove the thumb from the loop, and pull the tail to tighten the stitch; repeat from * once.

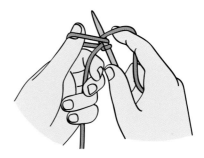

4. With another needle, lift the second stitch from the needle tip over the stitch closest to the tip and off the needle. Repeat from *.

Knotted Cast On: Guernsey Variation

Traditionally used on sweaters in Guernsey, this technique incorporates the backward-loop cast on. Beware: it's difficult to control the tension.

Knotted cast on: Guernsey variation

1. Cast on two stitches using the backward-loop cast on (page 14) as follows: Make a slipknot about 5" from the end of the yarn and put it on the right needle. *Holding the ball on the left and the tail in the right fingers, swing the left thumb behind and under the strand, and then forward and up to create a loop around the thumb. Insert the needle into the loop as if to knit then release the loop and pull yarn to tighten the stitch. Repeat from * once.
2. Work step 4 of the knotted cast on (above).
3. Repeat steps 1 and 2.

Knotted Cast On: Knit Variation

This is the knit cast on version.

Knotted cast on: knit variation

1. Make a slipknot about 5" from the end of the yarn and place it on the left needle. Cast on two stitches using the knit cast on (page 48) as follows: *knit the first stitch, but leave it on the left needle.

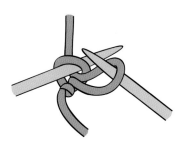

2. Rotate the right needle clockwise, insert the tip of the left needle into the loop from left to right, and remove the right needle; repeat from * once.

3. With the right needle, lift the second stitch over the stitch closest to the needle tip and off the needle. Repeat from *.

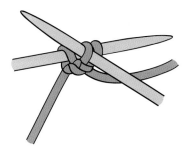

Double-Needle Cast On

Although appropriate for many projects, this cast on creates an extremely flexible edge that is particularly nice for lace patterns, especially those that produce deeply scalloped or wavy edges. It requires two needles, one at least two sizes smaller than the project needles.

Double-needle cast on

1. Leaving a long tail, make a slipknot and place it on the larger needle. Place the smaller needle under and parallel to the larger needle, with the slipknot between the needles. Insert the left thumb and index finger between the strands, spread them apart, and turn them up to wrap the tail around the thumb and the working yarn around the index finger. Hold both ends in the remaining fingers of the left hand.

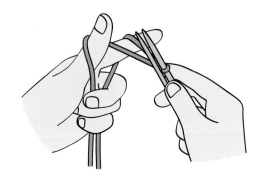

2. Insert both needle tips into the thumb loop as if to knit.

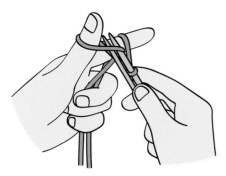

3. Swing the needles back and slip the front finger strand between the needles from back to front.

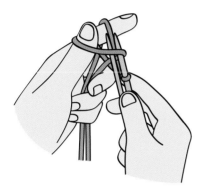

4. Swing the needles to the left behind the finger strand, and then back through the thumb loop and up.

5. Slip the front thumb strand between the needles from back to front, remove the thumb from the loop, insert it between the strands, and pull it toward you to tighten the stitch. There will be a new loop on each needle.

6. Keeping the two strands taut, rotate the needles together clockwise, down behind the strands, under them, and up to twist the strands under the smaller needle. Halfway through the rotation, the smaller needle will be on top of the larger needle.

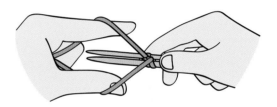

7. At the end of the rotation, the larger needle will be back on top.

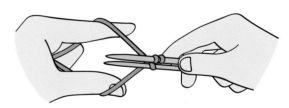

Repeat steps 2–7. Count only the stitches on the larger needle. When you have cast on the required number of stitches, pull out the smaller needle and begin your work. If you are working flat, the first row will be the wrong side. After several rows, if the edge is uneven with large loops, gently stretch it to ease out the loops.

Knit Cast Ons

Cast ons in this group use two needles and, as their name suggests, are worked as if you are knitting or purling. The knit cast on is often taught to beginners because it's so similar to actual knitting and is easy to learn. The knit cast ons can produce a tight edge, so they need to be worked slightly looser than you might think. Even so, the edges are less elastic than those of the long-tail cast ons. They also have a tendency to pull out of shape, especially if the tension is not uniform along the edge.

Unlike the long-tail cast ons (page 18), these techniques don't require a long tail, just 4" or 5", so there is no guessing about tail length.

Knit Cast On

Also called Knitting On, Two-Needle Cast On, Chain Cast On, Lace Cast On, Knitted Lace Cast On, Loose Knit Stitch Cast On, School Cast On, Open Knit Cast On

A reliable all-around cast on, this method creates a strong edge that wears well. It's particularly suitable for beginners, as it is very similar to knitting. It's a good cast on to use when you need to add stitches in the middle of a project, such as for buttonholes, steeks, and knitting from cuff to cuff. Lace knitters favor it for its slightly loopy, open edge. Since many other cast ons and bind offs are based on the knit cast on, becoming familiar with it will pay off.

Knit cast on

1. Make a slipknot about 5" from the end of the yarn and place it on the left needle. *Insert the right needle into the slipknot or stitch and knit it, but leave the stitch on the left needle.

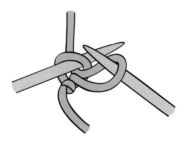

2. Rotate the right needle clockwise, insert the tip of the left needle into the stitch from left to right, and remove the right needle.

3. Repeat from *. On the last stitch, bring the working yarn to the front before slipping the stitch to the left needle to separate the last two stitches.

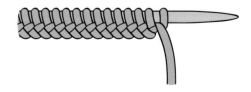

Knit Cast On: Woven Variation

Also called Woven Cast On

This variation creates a dense edge that is not elastic. It tends to be tight, so it is best to cast on with needles a size larger than the project needles to prevent puckering.

Knit cast on: woven variation

Cast on using the knit cast on (opposite). On the first row only, knit in the back of the stitches to twist them. Then knit normally.

Twice-Knitted Cast On

This variation of the knit cast on (opposite) creates a firm, nonelastic edge that is less likely to curl. It's a tight cast on, so work loosely. You will find it helpful to use needles at least one size larger than the project needles, although the first row of stitches will be elongated. Inserting the needle all the way up to the shaft before wrapping will also help.

Twice-knitted cast on

1. Make a slipknot about 5" from the end of the yarn and place it on the left needle. Cast on one stitch using the knit cast on (opposite) as follows: knit the first stitch, but leave the stitch on the left needle.

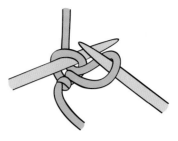

2. Rotate the right needle clockwise, insert the tip of the left needle into the loop from left to right, and remove the needle.

3. K2tog. Rotate the right needle clockwise, insert the left needle into the loop from left to right, and remove the right needle. Repeat this step.

Purled Cast On

This is the reverse of the knit cast on (page 48), with the right side on the opposite side and the strands slanting in the opposite direction. The tension is slightly easier to control, making this cast on easier to work than the knit cast on. The purled cast on is useful if you want the knit cast-on edge when working in the round.

Purled cast on

1. Make a slipknot about 5" from the end of the yarn and place it on the left needle. This is the first stitch.
2. *Purl the first stitch, but leave it on the left needle. Place the needle tips together, slip the stitch from the right to the left needle, and pull the yarn to tighten the stitch. Repeat from *.

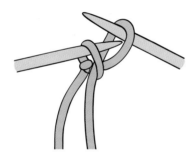

The first row is the wrong side if working flat.

Purled Cast On Variation

1. Make a slipknot about 5" from the end of the yarn and place it on the right needle. *Insert the left needle into the back of the stitch on the right needle from left to right, with the needle coming out on the far side.

2. With the yarn in front, purl the stitch, but leave it on the left needle.
3. Repeat from *. Every time you make a new stitch, the previous stitch will be transferred to the left needle. After casting on the last stitch, remove the right needle and pull the yarn to tighten the last stitch.

Knit-Purl Cast On

Achieve a K1, P1 edge by alternating the knit cast on (page 48) and the purled cast on (at left). This method can also be used for K2, P2 ribbing.

Knit-purl cast on

1. Make a slipknot about 5" from the end of the yarn and place it on the left needle. *Knit the first stitch, but leave it on the left needle.

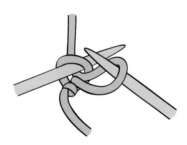

2. Rotate the right needle clockwise, insert the tip of the left needle into the stitch from left to right, and remove the right needle. Pull the yarn to tighten the stitch. This is the knit stitch.

3. Bring the right needle under the yarn to the back, and purl the first stitch, but leave it on the left needle. Place the needle tips together and slip the stitch from the right to the left needle. This is the purl stitch. Bring the needle under the yarn to the front.

4. Repeat from *, alternating knit and purl stitches. Begin the first row with P1.

For K2, P2 ribbing, work steps 1 and 2 twice to make two knit stitches before working step 3 twice for the two purl stitches.

Cable Cast On

Also called Lace Cast On, School Cast On, Firm Knit-Stitch Cast On

A variation of the knit cast on (page 48), this method creates a cable-like edge that is firmer and less elastic than the knit cast ons. To make a slightly more flexible edge, insert the needle up to the shaft, not just to the tip, before making the stitch. Also, if you insert the needle for the new stitch before tightening the stitch just made, you will achieve more even edges. This cast on can be used when adding stitches in the middle of your work—for example, for buttonholes and steeks, where the edges need to be firm.

Cable cast on

1. Make a slipknot about 5" from the end of the yarn and place it on the left needle. Cast on one stitch using the knit cast on (page 48) as follows: knit the first stitch, but leave it on the left needle.

2. Rotate the right needle clockwise, insert the left needle into the stitch from left to right, and remove the right needle.

3. Insert the right needle between the two stitches on the left needle.

4. Wrap the working yarn around the right needle as if to knit and pull the yarn back through the stitches. Rotate the right needle clockwise, insert the left needle into the loop from left to right, and remove the right needle. Pull the yarn to tighten the stitch.

5. Repeat steps 3 and 4, inserting the needle between the first two stitches on the left needle.

If you're adding on stitches in the middle of your project, start with step 3.

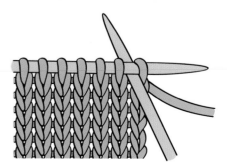

Purl Cable Cast On

This is the reverse of the cable cast on, with the right side of the edge on the opposite side and the strands slanting in the opposite direction. For a more even edge, insert the needle for the new stitch before tightening the stitch just made.

Purl cable cast on

1. Make a slipknot about 5" from the end of the yarn and place it on the left needle. Use the knit cast on (page 48) to cast on one stitch as follows: knit the first stitch, but leave it on the left needle.

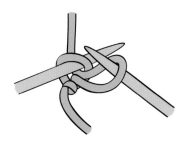

2. Rotate the right needle clockwise, insert the tip of the left needle into the stitch from left to right, and remove the right needle.

3. Insert the right needle from back to front between the two stitches on the left needle. With the yarn in front, wrap it around the right needle as if to purl, and pull the yarn through to the back.

4. Rotate the right needle clockwise, insert the left needle into the loop from left to right, and remove the right needle.

5. Repeat steps 3 and 4. The first row is the wrong side if working flat.

Alternate Cable Cast On

Also called Ribbed Cable Cast On, Rib Cable Cast On, Knit-Purl Cable Cast On

This cast on alternates the cable and the purl cable cast ons (page 51 and opposite). It creates a K1, P1 edge that is firm and good to use with K1, P1 ribbing or seed stitch. The edge is slightly stretchier than the cable cast-on edge.

Alternate cable cast on

1. Make a slipknot about 5" from the end of the yarn and place it on the left needle. Cast on one stitch using the knit cast on (page 48) as follows: knit the first stitch, but leave it on the left needle.

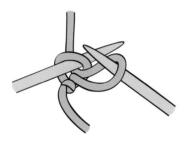

2. Rotate the right needle clockwise, insert the tip of the left needle into the stitch from left to right, and remove the right needle.

3. Bring the right needle under the yarn to the back and insert it from back to front between the two stitches on the left needle. With the yarn in front, wrap it around the right needle as if to purl, and pull the yarn through to the back.

4. Rotate the right needle clockwise, insert the left needle into the loop from left to right, and remove the right needle. This is the purl stitch.

5. Insert the right needle between the two stitches on the left needle.

6. Wrap the working yarn around the right needle as if to knit and pull the yarn through the stitches. Rotate the right needle clockwise, insert the left needle into the loop from left to right, and remove the right needle. Pull the yarn to tighten the stitch. This is the knit stitch.

7. Repeat steps 3–6. On the first row only, knit the knit stitches through the back loop. You can either purl the slipknot or drop it.

Chinese Waitress Cast On

My friend Mary Hu learned this cast on from a waitress in a Beijing restaurant. The double chain is split along the bottom edge, creating an identical appearance on both sides of the knitting. The edge is neat, decorative, and elastic. The stitches immediately above the edge are slightly elongated.

Chinese waitress cast on

1. Make a slipknot about 5" from the end of the yarn and place it on the left needle. Place the right needle under and perpendicular to the left needle, to the right of the slipknot.

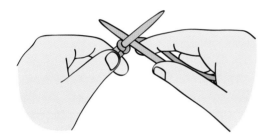

2. With the right fingers, bring the yarn forward, over the left needle from front to back, and wrap it around the right needle tip as if to knit.

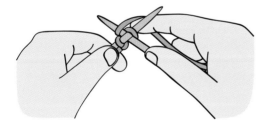

3. Pull the loop through and to the right.

4. Remove the right needle, being careful not to drop the loop.

5. Untwist the loop counterclockwise and reinsert the right needle into the loop.

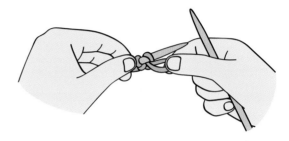

6. Place the right needle under and perpendicular to the left needle to the right of the last stitch on the left needle, bring the yarn forward, over the left needle from front to back, and wrap it around the right needle tip as if to knit.

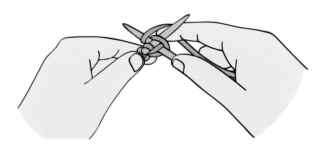

7. Pull the yarn through to the front and through the loop on the right needle.

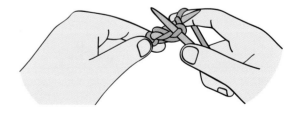

8. Repeat steps 4–7 until you have one less than the desired number of stitches. Slip the loop from the right needle to the left to create the final stitch.

Two-Color Cast Ons

These cast ons create decorative effects using two colors of yarn. There is a limit, however, to what two colors can achieve, so most of the edges produced by these cast ons are basically the same. The main difference is whether the slanting strands on the right side are all the contrasting color, which highlights the edge, or alternate between the main color and the contrasting color, which creates a braided effect. Another difference is that some of the cast ons make stitches that are all in the main color, while several make stitches that alternate between the main color and the contrasting color.

Long-Tail Two-Color Cast On

Also called One-Needle with Two Colors, Two-Color Cable Cast On

This cast on creates a line of contrasting color along the edge on the right side and bumps of contrasting color on the wrong side. All cast-on stitches are worked in the main color.

Long-tail two-color cast on

Make a slipknot with two strands of different colored yarn together about 5" from their ends and place the knot on the right needle. Cast on using either the continental or English method of the long-tail cast on (pages 19 and 20). The color of the yarn over the thumb will be the color of the bottom edge. Do not count the slipknot as a stitch. Remove it before starting to knit.

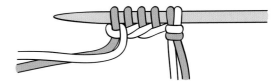

The first row is the wrong side if working flat.

Two-Color Cast On with Three Strands

Also called Double-Twist Cast On, Two-End Cast On

Used in Scandinavian twined knitting, this technique uses three strands—two of the main color and one of a contrasting color—to create a thicker, less flexible edge than the long-tail two-color cast on. The twining creates a different visual effect; the cast-on stitches are all the main color. This is a tight cast on, so work loosely.

Two-color cast on with three strands

1. Begin with three strands of yarn, two of a main color and one of a contrasting color. Use the three strands together to make a slipknot about 5" from the yarn ends and place the knot on the needle. Hold the needle in the right hand with the main-color balls of yarn on the right. Holding the contrasting-color strand in the left fingers, swing the left thumb over, behind, and under the contrasting yarn, and then up to create a loop on the thumb. Follow the long-tail cast on: English method (page 20), steps 2–4.

2. Drop the main-color strand you just used in front of the other working main-color strand. Cast on another stitch using the main-color strand that is now to the back.

Continue to alternate the main-color strands, always taking the main-color strand from the back. Do not count the slipknot as a stitch. Remove it before starting to knit.

The first row is the wrong side if working flat.

Two-Color Cast On with Three Strands Variation

Also called German Twisted Two-Color Cast On

This variation uses the German twisted cast on (page 34) instead of the basic long-tail cast on (page 18).

Two-color cast on with three strands variation

1. Measure out a long tail of the contrasting color. Place the end of the main-color yarn at the starting point of the contrasting color, make a slipknot with the two yarns together, and place it on the right needle. On the left you will have a long tail of the contrasting color and a short tail of the main color.

Both balls will be on the right. Always wrap the contrasting color around the thumb and alternate the main color and the contrasting color around the index finger for wrapping.

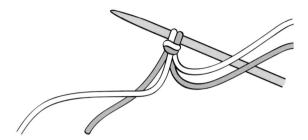

2. *Use the German twisted cast on English method (page 35) as follows: Cast on one stitch with the main-color strand, and drop this strand behind the contrasting-color strand. Cast on one stitch with the contrasting-color strand over the index finger (or the one used for wrapping). Repeat from *, always picking up the strand that is closest to you.

Dala-Floda Cast On

This Swedish cast on is very similar to the long-tail two-color cast on (page 55), but the contrasting-color strands slant in the opposite direction.

Dala-Floda cast on

1. Make a slipknot with two strands of different colored yarns together about 5" from their ends and place the knot on the left needle. *Bring the contrasting-color strand behind the main-color strand and wrap it over the needle from back to front.

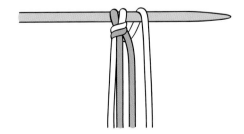

2. Bring the main-color strand in front of the contrasting-color strand and wrap it over the needle from back to front.

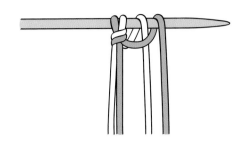

3. With the right needle, lift the contrasting-color loop on the needle over the main-color strand (closest to the needle tip) and off the needle. Pull both strands to tighten the stitch.

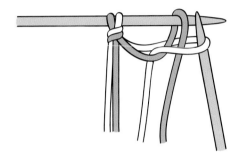

4. Repeat from *. Do not count the slipknot as a stitch. Drop it off the needle before working the first row. The first row is the wrong side if working flat.

Two-Color Cable Cast On

This variation of the cable cast on (page 51) produces an edge of slanting strands alternating in color; the stitches alternate in color as well. The edge is the same on both sides. This cast on tends to be tight, so work loosely.

Two-color cable cast on

1. Make a slipknot with two different colored yarns together about 5" from their ends and place the knot on the left needle. Arrange the loops of the knot so that the main color is on the left and the contrasting color is closest to the needle tip.
2. Insert the right needle between the two stitches from front to back. Wrap the main-color strand around the right needle as if to knit, and pull the loop through the two stitches. Rotate the right needle clockwise, insert the tip of the left needle into the stitch from left to right, and remove the right needle.

3. Insert the right needle between the first two stitches on the left needle from front to back. Rotate the working strands clockwise, use the contrasting color to wrap the yarn around the needle as if to knit, and pull the loop through. Slip the stitch purlwise from the right to the left needle.

4. Repeat steps 2 and 3, alternating the two colors. On the last stitch, bring the yarn to the front before slipping the stitch to the left needle. You can count the knot as two stitches, or you can undo the knot before starting to knit. Knit the first row in the main color to create the decorative effect.

Kihnu Troi Cast On

Also called Braided Cast On

Nancy Bush introduced the knitting world to this Estonian cast on. Characterized by a raised braid of two alternating colors along the bottom of the edge, this is a wonderful choice for mitten and sock cuffs. The cast-on stitches also alternate in color. Controlling the tension can be tricky, but with practice you'll get the hang of it.

Kihnu troi cast on

1. Make separate slipknots with two strands of different colored yarn about 5" from their ends. Place the knots on the left needle, with the darker color to the left of the lighter color. With the working strands in back, knit the light stitch on the left needle with the dark strand.

2. Bring both strands of working yarn to the front between the needles and place the dark strand on the right. Bring the light strand to the back between the needles and *wrap it clockwise around the needle to make a reverse yarn over (this is the opposite of the usual direction for a yarn over). Use this strand to knit the dark stitch on the left needle. Pull the front strand to tighten the stitch. Slip the stitch just made back to the left needle.

3. Bring the light strand to the front between the needles and place it on the right. Bring the dark strand under the light strand and to the back.

4. Repeat from *, alternating colors, until you have one more stitch than required. The last two stitches will be the same color. If working in the round, make sure they're the opposite color of the first stitch. When joining the work, slip the first stitch on the left needle to the right needle. Lift the last stitch (the second in from the needle tip) over the first stitch and off the needle. Slip the first stitch back to the left needle. The second colored stitch will be gone and the stitches will alternate in color. If working flat, end with step 2, bring the front strand to the back, and slip the stitch on the left needle to the right needle. For either, on the first row only, knit the stitches through the back loop.

Liidia's Braid Cast On

This is another Estonian cast on from Nancy Bush that creates a braid in alternating colors along the edge. The cast-on stitches also alternate in color, but the braid runs in the opposite direction from the Kihnu troi on page 59. It works best if you do not cast on too loosely.

Liidia's braid cast on

1. Make a slipknot with two different colored yarns together about 5" from their ends and place the knot on the needle. Hold the needle in the right hand and hold the strands taut in the left fingers. Insert the left index finger between the strands and swing it back and up to wrap the dark strand around it. Wrap the left thumb counterclockwise around the light strand to create a loop around the thumb.

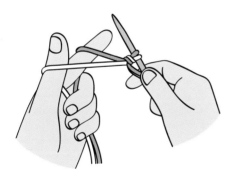

2. Insert the needle between the thumb strands and under the back thumb strand, catch the front index-finger strand from the right, and pull it back through the loop. Remove the thumb from the loop, insert it between the strands, and pull the strand toward you to tighten the stitch.

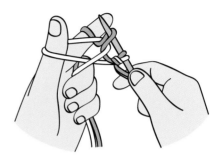

3. Rotate the two working strands, bringing the light strand under the dark strand, and wrap it around the left index finger, and then wrap the thumb counterclockwise around the dark strand.

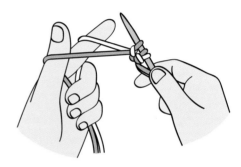

4. Repeat steps 2 and 3, alternating colors before making a new stitch. Do not count the slipknot as a stitch. Untie it before beginning to knit. The first row is the wrong side if working flat.

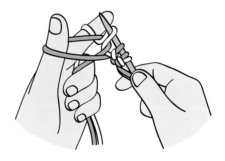

Decorative Cast Ons

While other cast ons do include some decorative elements, the methods in this miscellaneous group place a particular emphasis on decorative edges and do not easily fall into other categories.

Frilled Cast On

Also called Stretchy Cast On, Ruffled Cast On

As its name suggests, this is the solution when you want a gently frilly edge. It can be worked using a number of different cast ons, but it is more effective with some than with others. Likewise, it can look more attractive with some yarns than with others. Experiment to see what works best for your project.

Frilled cast on

1. Cast on twice the number of stitches required, using any of the loop or long-tail cast ons (pages 12 and 18).
2. On the next row, *K2tog; repeat from * to end. Begin your project on the next row.

Frilled Cast On: Purled Variation

This cast on creates the frilled edge on a purl row. Follow step 1 of the frilled cast on (above). On the next row, *P2tog; repeat from * to end.

Frilled Cast On: Ribbed Variation

Try this variation for ribbed patterns.

Frilled cast on: ribbed variation

Follow step 1 of the frilled cast on (at left), but make the stitch count a multiple of four. On the next row, *K2tog, P2tog; repeat from * to end.

Frilled Cast On: Ruffled Variation

This deeper, more gently ruffled edge is most effective when created with energized singles (highly spun, single-ply yarns). You can use this variation with most of the loop or long-tail cast ons (pages 12 and 18).

Frilled cast on: ruffled variation

1. Follow step 1 of the frilled cast on (at left).
2. Knit four rows in stockinette stitch.
3. On the next row, *K2tog; repeat from * to end. Begin your project on the next row.

Frill-Edge Cast On

This cast on also creates a frilly edge by casting on more stitches than needed and then binding off or decreasing stitches on subsequent rows. You can use any of a number of different cast ons, and like the frilled cast on (page 61), it can be more effective with some cast ons and yarns than others. The edge is thicker than that of the frilled cast on and is frillier due to the larger number of stitches cast on.

Frill-edge cast on

1. Using the cast-on method of your choice, cast on four times the number of stitches required, minus three stitches. For example, if your pattern calls for 48 stitches, cast on 189 stitches.
   (48 x 4 = 192; 192 – 3 = 189)
2. On the next row: K1, *K2, lift the second stitch on the right needle over the one closest to the tip and off the needle; repeat from *.
3. On the next row: P1, *P2tog; repeat from *. Begin your project on the next row.

Fringe Cast On

This variation of the long-tail cast on comes from Estonia, and Nancy Bush once again deserves the credit for introducing it to the international knitting community.

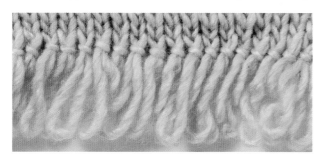

Fringe cast on

1. Leaving a long tail, make a slipknot and place it on the needle. Hold the needle in the right hand with both strands in the left fingers. *Insert the left thumb and index finger between the strands, spread

them apart, and turn them up to wrap the tail around the thumb and the working yarn around the index finger. Hold both ends in the remaining fingers of the left hand.

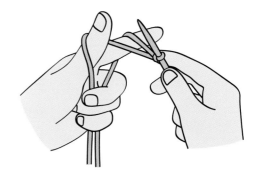

2. Insert the needle into the thumb loop as if to knit.

3. Swing the needle over, behind, and under both finger strands.

4. Catch both strands and pull them forward through the thumb loop.

5. Keeping the yarn wrapped around the finger, remove the thumb from the thumb loop and tighten the stitch by pulling the thumb strand and the finger loop. (The yarn around the finger creates the fringe, so make sure the loop is the same length for each stitch.)

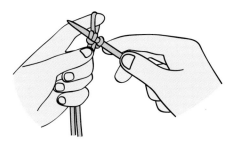

6. Remove the finger from the loop.

7. Repeat from *. The cast-on stitches will be two strands of yarn. On the next row, knit each pair together as one stitch.

Fringe Cast On: Two-Color Variation

Holding two different colored yarns together, make a slipknot about 5" from their ends and place it on the needle. Then follow the steps for the fringe cast on (opposite). After making the first stitch, reverse the position of the strands by rotating the strands clockwise close to the needle. Repeat, alternating the color of the fringe loops.

Chain Cast On

Also called Chain-Edge Cast On, Chained Cast On, Bind-Off Cast On, Japanese Cast On, Cast-Off Cast On
This cast on creates an elastic edge with chained loops along the front. It resembles the standard bind-off edge (page 114) and can be used with it when you want the cast-on and bound-off edges to look the same. You will need a crochet hook as well as a needle. The size of the hook is not too important, as the needle will determine the size of the stitches.

Chain cast on

1. Make a loose slipknot about 5" from the end of the yarn and place it on the crochet hook. Hold the hook in your right hand and the needle in your left hand. Loop the working strand over the left index finger. *With the crochet hook above the needle and the working yarn below it, swing the hook from the left behind the strand on the index finger, catch the yarn, and pull the loop over the needle and through the slipknot.

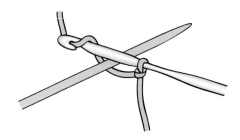

2. Bring the working yarn to the back under the needle.

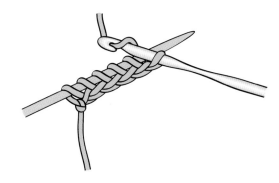

3. Repeat from * until there is one less stitch than required. Slip the remaining loop from the hook to the needle.

Chained Cast On

Using two needles instead of a crochet hook and a needle, this method creates the same edge as the chain cast on (page 63). The edge is elastic and useful when you need to add stitches in the middle of a project—for example, when using steeks or knitting a garment from cuff to cuff. It's an extremely loose cast on, so use needles at least four sizes smaller than the project needles to keep the edge tight and tidy.

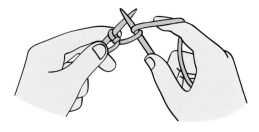

Chained cast on

1. Make a slipknot about 5" from the end of the yarn and place it on the left needle. Hold the working strand taut in the right fingers.
2. *Wrap the yarn counterclockwise around the right needle, and purl the stitch on the left needle.

3. With the yarn in front, place the needle tips together and slip the stitch just made back to the left needle.

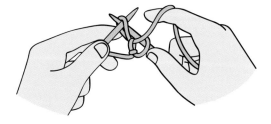

4. Repeat from *, ending with step 2.

Chained Cast On Variation
Also called Chain Loop Cast On

This variation creates an expandable edge by inserting a stitch between each cast-on stitch. It is particularly useful with lace stitches that produce a very wavy, pointed, or scalloped edge.

Chained cast on variation

Work steps 1–3 of Chained Cast On (at left). To lengthen the edge at any point, repeat step 3 however many times you want before continuing the cast on.

Decorative Cast Ons

I-Cord Cast On

An I-cord is a narrow knitted tube that can serve many different functions in knitting. As part of a cast on, it creates a neat, clean edge. This cast on is worked on double-pointed needles. You can make the cord bigger or smaller by increasing or decreasing the number of stitches used to make it; generally, three to five stitches are used. Pair it with the I-cord bind off (page 125) for matching edges.

I-Cord Cast On 1

Here you will knit the I-cord first, and then pick up the required cast-on stitches along the side of the I-cord.

I-cord cast on 1

1. To make an I-cord on double-pointed needles, cast on three stitches (or another number, if desired) using any cast-on method. Knit one row. Do not turn. *Slide the stitches to the other end of the needle, pull the yarn around the back of your work fairly tightly, and knit the three stitches; repeat from * to create the cord.

2. Make the cord as long as the width of the piece being cast on. Break the yarn and thread the tail through the loops of all the stitches, pull tight, and fasten off. (You can also put the three stitches onto a stitch holder so that you can make an attached I-cord up the side of the piece.)

3. With a knitting needle, pick up and knit the required number of stitches through the side loops of stitches along the side of the I-cord. Make sure you pick up along the same row of stitches so that the edge will be even.

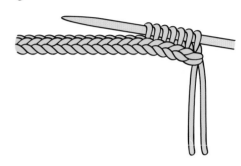

I-Cord Cast On 2

This method creates the I-cord as you cast on stitches. You can increase the size of the I-cord by initially casting on more stitches and always slipping that number of stitches each time. The first row of stitches will be slightly elongated.

I-cord cast on 2

1. Cast on four stitches using any cast-on method. Slip the stitches from the right to the left needle as if to purl.
2. Knit into the front and back of the first stitch to make two stitches, and knit the next three stitches.
3. Slip the first four stitches back to the left needle and pull the yarn snug.
4. Repeat steps 2 and 3 until you have the required number of stitches plus the four I-cord stitches, ending with step 2. Turn and bind off the four I-cord stitches. Then work across the first row, the wrong side.

Edging Cast On

This cast on is worked much like the I-cord and picot chain cast ons (pages 65 and 70), making a narrow strip along the edge in which stitches are picked up. The strip can be stockinette stitch, as illustrated here, a decorative pattern, or a lace panel as shown in the photo.

The number of rows in the strip will not necessarily correspond directly with the number of stitches to be picked up. Knit a swatch to determine the length of the strip needed to accommodate the number of stitches called for in your pattern. You can also make the strip much longer and pucker it when picking up stitches to create a frilled edge. Pair this cast on with the edging bind off (page 126) for matching edges.

Edging cast on

1. Using the cast-on method of your choice, cast on the required number of stitches for your edging pattern. Knit a narrow strip in your pattern as long as the width of the edge to be cast on. Bind off the stitches, leaving the last stitch on the needle.

2. Turn the strip so that it is horizontal and the needle is on the right. Pick up and knit the required number of stitches along the edge of the strip.

CAST ONS

Three-Strand Cast On

Used in Scandinavian twined knitting, this technique can be worked with three strands of the same color or three different colors. To learn it, you may find it easier to use three different colors.

Three-strand cast on in one color

Three-strand cast on in multiple colors

1. Make a slipknot with three strands of yarn together about 5" from the end of the strands and place the knot on the needle. Hold the needle in the left hand. Separate the strands so that strand 1 is on the right, strand 2 is in the middle, and strand 3 is on the left.

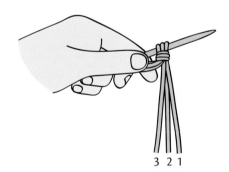

2. Wrap strand 1 over the left index finger and needle from back to front, and then bring strand 3 in front of strand 1 and wrap it over the needle from back to front.

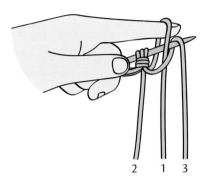

3. Loosely hold strand 3 in the right fingers while lifting the index-finger loop over the strand 3 loop and off the needle. Pull strands 1 and 3 to tighten the stitch.

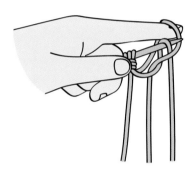

   Strand 1 is now strand 2, strand 2 is now strand 3, and strand 3 is now strand 1.

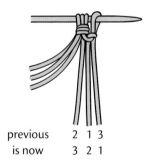

4. Repeat steps 2 and 3. Once you have cast on, untie the slipknot. The first row is the wrong side if working flat.

Peruvian Cast On

From Peru by way of Montse Stanley, this cast on creates an edge featuring tiny eyelets. Controlling the tension can be difficult until you get the hang of it.

Peruvian cast on

1. Hold the end of the yarn securely in the left fingers with the ball on the right. Make a slipknot by wrapping the yarn around the left index and middle fingers from front to back.

2. Push the working strand through the loop around the fingers from back to front.

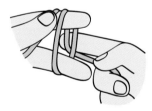

3. Insert the right index finger into the newly created loop from front to back.

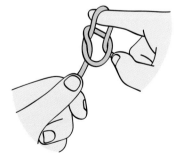

4. Insert the needle into the knot's circle from back to front and pull the tail to tighten the stitch on the needle, keeping the loop on the finger.

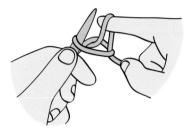

5. Place the index-finger loop on the needle with the nonslipping side of the loop to the back.

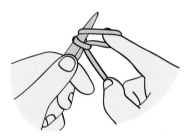

6. Hold the working strand in the left fingers. With the right fingers, pull the working strand through the loop on the needle from the back to create a new loop. Insert the right index finger into the new loop to tighten the stitch.

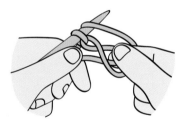

7. Repeat steps 5 and 6, ending with step 5, and pull the strand snug. If the finger loop gets too long, pull the working strand.

Decorative Cast Ons

Picot Cast On

Picot means "little point" in French, indicating the pronounced picot points created by this cast on. The length and spacing of the points can be adjusted by changing how many stitches are cast on and bound off, as long as the number of stitches cast on is greater than the number bound off. This cast on is not appropriate for thick, bulky, or novelty yarns; also, if the picots are placed too close together, the edge will tend to pucker. Pair the picot cast ons with the picot bind offs (page 126) for matching edges.

Picot cast on

1. Make a slipknot about 5" from the end of the yarn and place it on the left needle. Cast on six stitches using the knit cast on (page 48) as follows: *Knit the first stitch, but leave it on the left needle.

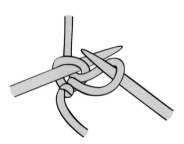

2. Rotate the right needle clockwise, insert the tip of the left needle into the stitch from left to right, and remove the right needle; repeat from * five times.

3. Bind off three stitches using the standard bind off (page 114) as follows: K2, with the left needle, lift the right stitch over the left and off the needle. Repeat this step twice, knitting one stitch instead of two.
4. Place the needle tips together and slip the stitch on the right needle to the left needle. Repeat from *.

Picot Chain Cast On

Also called Lace Cast On, Eyelet Cast On

Here is a lovely cast-on option for lace, especially patterns with very wavy, scalloped, or pointed edges. The edge is elastic, with open loops that complement most lace stitches, and a long lacy strip is produced that becomes the bottom edge. You can control the size of the loops by choosing a larger or smaller needle for the cast on.

Picot chain cast on

1. Make a slipknot about 5" from the end of the yarn and place it on the left needle. Knit the first stitch, but keep it on the left needle.

2. Rotate the right needle clockwise, insert the tip of the left needle into the loop from left to right, and remove the right needle. There are now two stitches on the left needle.

3. With the yarn in front, slip one stitch as if to purl from the left to the right needle and knit the next stitch on the left needle, creating a yarn over. Make sure the yarn over stays to the right of the slipped stitch.

4. With the left needle, lift the slipped stitch (the middle stitch) over the knit stitch and off the needle. Turn the work.

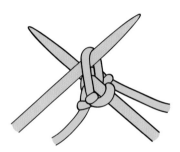

5. Repeat steps 3 and 4 until the picot chain has the same number of side loops as stitches to be cast on. Then repeat steps 3 and 4 once more without the yarn over, leaving one stitch on the needle. You will have a long chain with loops alternating on both sides.

Turn the chain so that it is horizontal, and pick up and knit a stitch in each picot loop along one edge.

Picot Chain Cast On: Eyelet Variation

Also called Eyelet Cast On

The picot loops here are much less pronounced on the edge.

Picot chain cast on: eyelet variation

1. Make a slipknot about 5" from the end of the yarn and place it on the right needle. Hold the needle in the right hand with the ball on the right. Holding the tail in the left fingers, cast on one stitch using the long-tail cast on: English method (page 20) as follows: swing the left thumb over, behind, and under the tail to wrap the strand around the thumb.

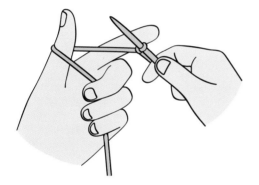

2. Insert the needle into the thumb loop as if to knit.

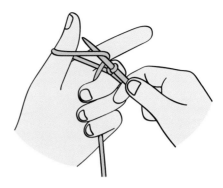

3. Wrap the working yarn around the needle as if to knit, and pull the strand through the thumb loop. Remove the thumb from the loop and pull the tail to tighten the stitch. Turn.

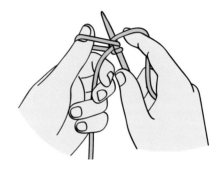

4. With the yarn in front to create a yarn over, insert the right needle into the back loop of both stitches on the left needle and knit them together. Be sure to work loosely. Turn.
5. Repeat step 4 until the strip has the same number of loops on both sides as stitches to be cast on. Then repeat step 4 once more without the yarn over, leaving one stitch on the needle. Turn the chain so that it is horizontal, and pick up and knit a stitch in each picot loop along one edge.

Picot Ribbing Cast On

Also called Picot Cast On, Picot Rib Cast On, Alternating Cast On

Small picot points are offset by indentations along the edge. This method is best suited for a K1, P1 ribbing.

Picot ribbing cast on

1. Leaving a long tail, make a slipknot and place it on the needle. Hold the needle in the right hand with both strands in the left hand. Insert the left thumb and index finger between the strands, spread them apart, and turn them up to wrap the tail around the thumb and the working yarn around the index finger. Hold both ends in the fingers of the left hand.

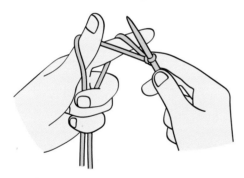

2. Swing the needle forward, down, and under the thumb strand.

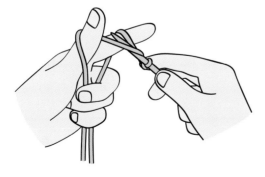

3. Bring the needle up and over the finger strand to catch it.

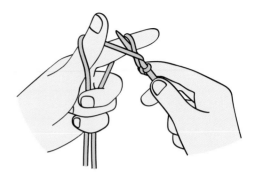

4. Pull the strand forward, under the thumb strand, and up. This is the knit stitch.

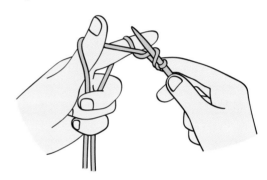

5. Cast on one stitch using the long-tail cast on: continental method (page 19) as follows: insert the needle tip into the thumb loop as if to knit.

Decorative Cast Ons

6. Catch the front strand on the index finger with the needle from the right and pull it back through the thumb loop. Remove the thumb from the loop, insert it between the strands, and pull the tail toward you to tighten the stitch. This is the purl stitch.

7. Repeat steps 2–6. Work the first row in K1, P1 ribbing, beginning with K1.

Slipknot Cast On

This cast on creates a row of slipknots along the flexible, open edge. If you want a tighter edge, knit through the back of the stitches on the first row only. Both sides of the edge look the same. You may find it challenging to get the tension right when first learning this cast on.

Slipknot cast on

1. Make a slipknot about 5" from the end of the strand and place it on the needle. With the needle in the right hand, hold the yarn taut between both hands, with the ball on the left and the tail in the right fingers. *Swing the left index finger in front of the yarn, under it, and up to wrap the yarn around the finger.

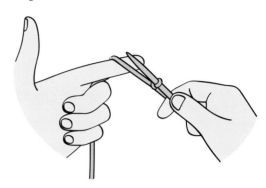

2. Crook the finger and move the tip to the left, creating a loop on the finger. Insert the needle into the loop as if to purl.

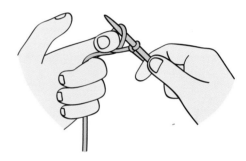

3. Remove the finger from the loop and hold the left side of the loop between the left thumb and index finger. Bring the needle forward, under the working strand and up to catch it, and pull it back through the loop. Slide the new stitch close to the previous one on the right needle and hold it in place with the right index finger as you pull the yarn to tighten the stitch. Repeat from *.

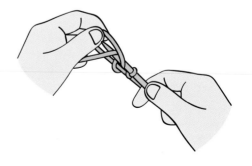

Double Cast On

With a row of slipknots along the bottom edge, this edge looks slightly different from that created by the slipknot cast on (page 73), and the tension is a bit easier to control. It looks the same on both sides and is good with the garter stitch.

Double cast on

1. With the ball of yarn on the right, drape the tail over the left index finger from back to front, and then wrap it clockwise around the left thumb and hold the end in the remaining fingers of the left hand with the working end.

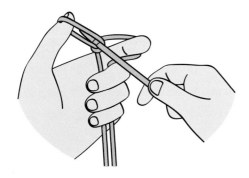

2. Insert the needle into the thumb loop as if to knit, and swing the needle to the right of and behind the front finger strand to catch it.

3. Pull the strand through the thumb loop. Place the right index finger on top of the loop on the needle, remove the thumb from the loop, and pull both strands to tighten the stitch.

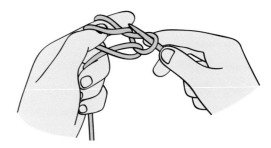

4. Hold the working strand between the left pinky and fourth finger, drape the working yarn over the left index finger from back to front, and wrap the yarn clockwise around the left thumb.

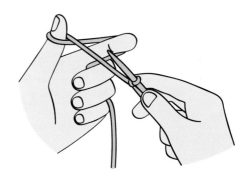

5. Repeat steps 2–4, sliding the new stitch close to the previously made stitch on the right needle and holding it in place with the right index finger as you pull the strand to tighten the stitch.

CAST ONS

Tubular Cast Ons

This group of cast ons creates a neat, rounded edge. There is no ridge along the bottom, so the cast-on edge seems to virtually disappear, much like on commercial knitwear. As a result, some knitters refer to tubular cast ons as "invisible cast ons." You can pair them with the tubular bind offs (page 150) for matching edges.

Tubular cast ons are often confused with provisional cast ons, possibly because they both use waste yarn. However, they have totally different purposes.

Tubular cast ons produce a very strong, elastic edge that is particularly well suited for K1, P1 ribbing. Although they can be used for K2, P2 ribbing, the resulting edge is not quite as even or consistent, nor usually as stretchy. Tubular cast ons can also be used for other knitting and will prevent an edge done in stockinette stitch from curling.

Tubular cast ons are not good for bulky yarns, as the bottom edge may end up being loose and flare out. If you find the edge too loose, try using smaller needles, but this will probably cause a decrease in elasticity.

There are numerous ways to achieve the tubular edge. Some cast ons use waste yarn. For these, choose a waste yarn that is about the same thickness as the project yarn. It should be strong, smooth, and slippery so that you can pull it out easily. Cotton is a good choice. Avoid fuzzy yarns as they will be harder to remove and may leave fibers behind that can detract from your project.

To remove the waste yarn, carefully snip it at one side of your knitting. Insert the tip of a needle into the loop of waste yarn and gently pull it loose. Then move to the next loop and pull it out. Continue across the bottom edge. Snipping the waste yarn frequently along the edge will make its removal much easier. If you use a strong, slippery yarn, you may be able to simply pull it out without snipping.

Double knitting is involved in most of the tubular cast ons, helping to create the rounded edge. Double knitting is a way of knitting two layers of fabric simultaneously on two needles. The stitches of the two layers alternate on the needles. Each layer is worked on alternate rows: the stitches of layer one are knit on one row while the stitches of layer two are slipped. On the next row, this is reversed, with the stitches of layer one slipped and the stitches of layer two knit. In this way, you can knit two layers forming a doubly thick fabric or an open tube. It is possible that tubular cast ons were originally created to knit a tube, hence the use of double knitting. They were subsequently adapted to flat knitting, although many of these cast ons retained several rows of double knitting before starting the ribbing.

If you find that the edge stitches are not the same size as the ribbing stitches, try using needles two sizes larger when working the waste-yarn portion of the cast on. Switch to the project needles when beginning the ribbing. This may also make the edge more elastic.

Tubular Cast On
for K1, P1 Rib

Also called Invisible Cast On

This cast on is best for ribbing on flat pieces because you need easy access to the wrong side of the fabric. It creates a very elastic edge well suited to K1, P1 ribbing.

Tubular cast on for K1, P1 rib

1. With waste yarn, cast on half the number of stitches required using any cast on. Knit and purl a row using the waste yarn. Change to the project yarn and work three more rows of stockinette stitch, ending with a knit row.
2. On the next row (wrong side), P1, and with the tip of the right needle pick up the first loop of the project yarn from the isolated row just below where the waste yarn ended: count down three bumps below the strand between the needles and insert the needle into the loop from above.

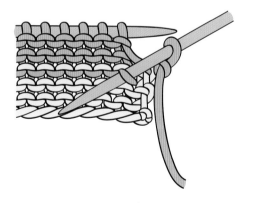

3. Place the loop on the left needle, bring the yarn to the back, and knit the loop. Purl the next stitch on the left needle, and pick up the next loop from the same row as before. Repeat this step, ending P1.

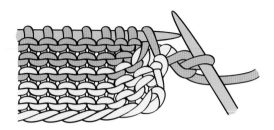

4. Begin K1, P1 ribbing, increasing one stitch by knitting into the front and back of the last stitch if an even number of stitches is required. After several rows, remove the waste yarn.

Tubular Cast On
for K2, P2 Rib

A tighter, less flexible edge is created by this cast on.

Tubular cast on for K2, P2 rib

1. Work step 1 of the tubular cast on for K1, P1 rib (above).
2. For steps 2–4, P2 instead of P1, and then pick up two loops in succession instead of one. Continue purling two and picking up two across, ending by picking up one and knitting in the front and back of the stitch.
3. Begin K2, P2 ribbing.

Stockinette Stitch Tubular Cast On

Although this cast on can be used for K2, P2 ribbing, the edge is tight and not as flexible as that of some other tubular cast ons. You will need waste yarn and a crochet hook.

Stockinette stitch tubular cast on

1. With waste yarn, make a slipknot about 5" from the end of the yarn and place it on a crochet hook. Make a loose chain consisting of half the number of chains as stitches required, plus a few more. Cut the waste yarn and pull the tail through the last chain to loosely secure the chain, or elongate the last chain.
2. Starting with the second chain from the end, use the project yarn and needles to pick up and knit one stitch through the back bump of each chain until you have half the number of required stitches on the needle. Work three rows of stockinette stitch, starting with a purl row.

3. Remove the tail from the last chain, carefully pull out the crochet chain, and pick up the live stitches on a second needle. The same number of stitches is on both needles.

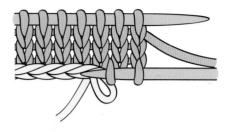

4. Fold the work by bringing the lower needle behind the top needle with the wrong sides facing. With a third needle, K1 from the front needle, and then P1 from the back needle. Continue alternating knitting a stitch from the front needle and purling a stitch from the back needle across the row.

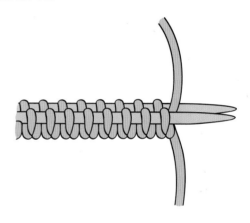

5. Work in K1, P1 ribbing.

Stockinette Stitch Tubular Cast On: K1, P1 Variation

This variation is tedious and slow, but the payoff is a nice edge. It requires a needle two sizes smaller than the project needle as well as waste yarn.

1. With waste yarn and the project needle, cast on half the number of stitches required using any method. Purl one row.

2. Knit the next row, wrapping the yarn around the needle twice for each stitch. Switch to the project yarn and on the next (wrong side) row, purl the first loop of each stitch and drop the second loop.

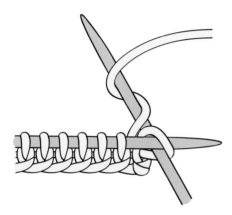

3. Work three rows in stockinette stitch, starting with a knit row. There will be a row of elongated stitches at the top of the waste yarn.

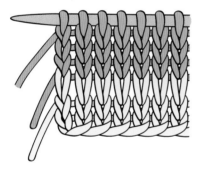

4. On the next row (wrong side), use a smaller needle to pick up the loops of the project yarn that join the tops of the elongated stitches by inserting the needle into the loops from above. The two needles are now parallel to each other, with one less stitch on the smaller needle.

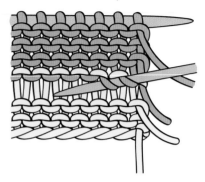

5. With the wrong side facing, alternate purling one stitch from the original needle and then knitting one from the small needle across the row.

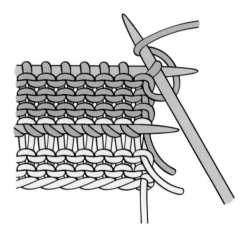

6. Begin K1, P1 ribbing, increasing one stitch by knitting into the front and back of the last stitch. After working several rows, remove the waste yarn.

Stockinette Stitch Tubular Cast On: K2, P2 Variation

Stockinette stitch tubular cast on: K2, P2 variation

1. Work steps 1–4 of stockinette stitch tubular cast on: K1, P1 variation (above), casting on half the number of required stitches plus one.
2. For step 5, work K2, P2 ribbing: P2 from the original needle, and then K2 from the smaller needle. You should end up with two stitches on the original needle and one on the smaller needle. P1, and then purl the last stitch on the original needle with the last stitch on the smaller one.
3. Continue in K2, P2 ribbing.

Yarn-Over Tubular Cast On 1

Also called Invisible Cast On, Casting On in Kitchener Rib

Using waste yarn and double knitting, this cast on produces an edge considerably looser and stretchier than some tubular edges.

Yarn-over tubular cast on 1

1. With waste yarn, cast on half the number of stitches required using any method. Cut the waste yarn. Turn.
2. Using the project yarn, K1, *bring the yarn to the front to form a yarn over, K1; repeat from *. If you're knitting in the round, end with a yarn over.
3. Begin double knitting.
   Working flat:
   Row 1: *Slip 1 purlwise with yarn in front, K1; repeat from * to last stitch, slip 1 purlwise.
   Row 2: K1, *slip 1 purlwise with yarn in front, K1; repeat from *.
   Repeat rows 1 and 2. K2tog at beginning of row before beginning ribbing.
   Working in the round:
   Round 1: *K1, slip 1 purlwise with yarn in front; repeat from *.
   Round 2: *Slip 1 purlwise with yarn in back, P1; repeat from *.
   Repeat rounds 1 and 2.
4. Begin K1, P1 ribbing. After working a few rows of ribbing, remove the waste yarn.

Yarn-Over Tubular Cast On 1 Variation

This requires three sets of needles, one four sizes smaller than the project needles and the other two sizes smaller. The smaller needles help to keep the edge from flaring out.

Work steps 1 and 2 of the yarn-over tubular cast on 1 with the largest needles, and then switch to the smallest needles for step 3. Change to the project needles for the repeat of rows 1 and 2.

Yarn-Over Tubular Cast On 2

Also called Casting On in Kitchener Rib, Chain Cast On
   This cast on creates a very loose, stretchy edge. It requires a crochet hook as well as waste yarn and involves double knitting.

Yarn-over tubular cast on 2

1. Using a crochet hook and waste yarn, make a chain with the same number of chains as stitches required, plus a few extras. Cut the waste yarn and loosely pull the end through the last loop to loosely secure the chain, or elongate the last chain.
2. With the project yarn, make a slipknot about 5" from the end of the yarn. Insert the needle through the back bump of the first chain and place the slipknot on the needle.

3. Pull the loop of the slipknot through the chain.

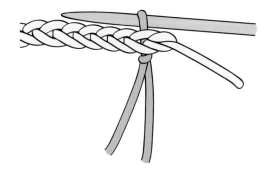

4. Bring the yarn to the front to make a yarn over, then skip one chain and pick up and knit a stitch in the back bump of the next chain.
5. Repeat step 4 until you have the required number of stitches, ending with a yarn over if you are knitting in the round or a picked-up stitch if working flat. If working flat, you'll have one more stitch than required.

On the next row, begin double knitting.

Working flat:
Row 1: *Slip 1 purlwise with yarn in front, K1; repeat from * to last stitch, slip 1.
Row 2: K1, *slip 1 purlwise with yarn in front, K1; repeat from *.
Repeat rows 1 and 2. K2tog at beginning of row before beginning your pattern.

Working in the round:
Round 1: *K1, slip 1 purlwise with yarn in front; repeat from *.
Round 2: *Slip 1 purlwise with yarn in back, P1; repeat from *.
Repeat rounds 1 and 2.

6. Begin K1, P1 ribbing. After working a few rows of ribbing, remove the waste yarn.

Tubular Cast On
for Double Rib

Also called 2 x 2 Tubular Cast On

This variation of the yarn-over tubular cast on 1 (page 79) is used for K2, P2 ribbing and creates a very loose, stretchy edge. It requires waste yarn and involves double knitting.

Tubular cast on for double rib

1. With waste yarn, cast on half the number of stitches required using any method. Cut the waste yarn.
2. Using the project yarn, K1, *bring the yarn to the front to form a yarn over, K1; repeat from * until you have the required number of stitches. If working flat, you'll have an extra stitch. If you're knitting in the round, end with a yarn over.
3. Begin double knitting.
   Working flat:
   Row 1: *Slip 1 purlwise with yarn in front, K1; repeat from * to last stitch, slip 1 purlwise.
   Row 2: K1, *slip 1 purlwise with yarn in front, K1; repeat from *.
   Repeat rows 1 and 2. K2tog when starting step 4. Cross two stitches to create the K2, P2 ribbing.
   Working in the round:
   Round 1: *K1, slip 1 purlwise with yarn in front; repeat from *.
   Round 2: *Slip 1 purlwise with yarn in back, P1; repeat from *.
   Repeat rounds 1 and 2.
   Cross two stitches to create the K2, P2 ribbing.
4. *K1, drop the next (purl) stitch from the needle to the back of the work, K1.

5. Slip the dropped purl stitch back on the left needle and purl it, P1; repeat from *.

OR

4. **K1, bring the needle in front of the next purl stitch, and knit the next knit stitch, but leave it on the needle.

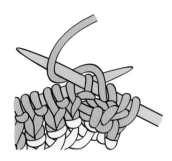

5. Bring the yarn to the front, purl the purl stitch, drop both stitches from the left needle, P1; repeat from **.

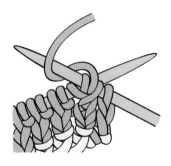

After repeating either rendition of steps 4 and 5 to cross stitches, continue in K2, P2 ribbing. After several rows, remove the waste yarn.

Two-Strand Tubular Cast On

Also called Kitchener Rib Cast On, Invisible Cast On, Italian Cast On, Tubular Cast On, KP Cast On, 1 x 1 Rib Cast On, Alternating Cast On

A nicely rhythmical cast on, this is very fast once you learn it. It involves double knitting. Keep the tension even on both strands to ensure they cross under the needle.

Two-strand tubular cast on

1. Leaving a long tail, make a slipknot and place it on the needle. Holding the needle in the right hand and both strands in the left hand, insert the left thumb and index finger between the strands, spread them apart, and turn them up so that the tail is wrapped around the thumb and the working yarn around the index finger. You may need to place your right index finger on top of the slipknot to hold it in place.

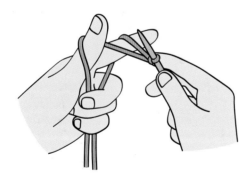

2. Bring the needle over the thumb strand, down under it, and up between the strands.

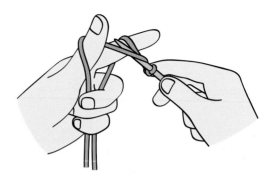

3. Bring the needle over the finger strand and back under it.

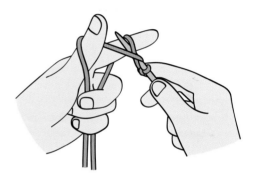

4. Bring the needle under the thumb strand and up to create a knit stitch.

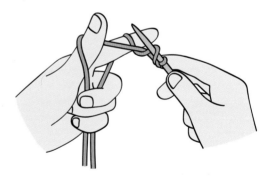

5. Bring the needle over, behind, and under the index-finger strand, and then forward and up between the two strands.

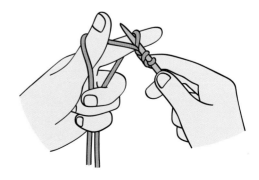

CAST ONS

6. Bring the needle over the thumb strand, down, and back under both strands. Bring the needle up to create a purl stitch on the needle.

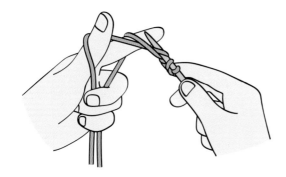

Repeat steps 2–6 until you have the required number of stitches. Do not count the slipknot as a stitch. Turn, wrap the tail counterclockwise around the working strand to secure the last stitch, and hold it in the left fingers.

7. Double knit for four rows, dropping the slipknot at the end of the first row.

Working flat:

K1, *slip 1 purlwise with yarn in front, K1 through the back loop for the first row only; repeat from * to last stitch (slipknot), ending slip 1, and then drop the slipknot off the needle. Repeat this row, knitting all stitches normally, ending slip 1 purlwise.

Working in the round:

Round 1: *K1 through the back loop, slip 1 purlwise with yarn in front; repeat from *. Knitting through the back loops on the first round only, *K1, sl 1 purlwise with yarn in front; repeat from * to the slipknot and drop it off the needle.

Round 2: *Slip 1 purlwise with yarn in front, P1; repeat from *.

Repeat rounds 1 and 2. Begin K1, P1 ribbing.

Two-Strand Tubular Cast On: Two-Color Variation

Also called Tubular Two-Color Cast On, Two-Color Italian Cast On

This variation, courtesy of Lynne Barr, uses double knitting to make a seamless tube on two needles. Each side can be a different color; the color change takes place along the tubular edge. Use double-pointed or circular needles so that you can slide the stitches from one end to the other.

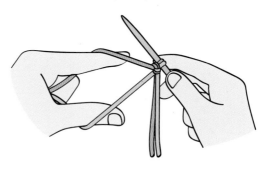

Two-strand tubular cast on: two-color variation

1. Make a slipknot with two different colored strands together about 5" from their ends. Place the slipknot on the right needle and follow steps 2–6 of the two-strand tubular cast on (at left).

2. Begin double knitting.

Row 1: With the color for this side (the color of the first stitch), *K1 through the back loop, slip 1 purlwise with yarn in front; repeat from * to the last stitch (slipknot). Drop the slipknot, but do not untie it. Do not turn. Slide the stitches to the other end of the needle.

Row 2: With the other color: *slip 1 purlwise with yarn in back, P1; repeat from *. Turn.

Continue double knitting rows 1 and 2 on each side, one for each color, before turning. After several rows, untie the slipknot.

The Family Treasure Cast On

This cast on involves double knitting and creates the same edge as the two-strand tubular cast on (page 82), but in a totally different way. I learned it from Mary Scott Huff, who says it has been used in her family ever since her mother found it in a European magazine in the 1940s. While learning this cast on, using long straight needles is best. Once you have mastered it, you can do it on circular needles.

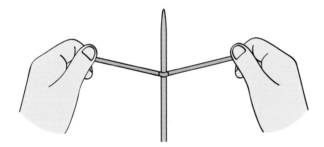

The family treasure cast on

1. Leaving a long tail, make a slipknot and place it on the needle. Hold the needle between your knees or in the crease of your hip to free up both hands. Hold the tail strand in your left fingers and the working strand in your right.

2. Bring the right strand under the needle, then up and over it from left to right. Bring the left strand under the needle, then up and over it from right to left.

3. Bring the right strand back over the needle, to the left of it, down, and under it.

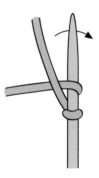

4. Bring the strand back up to the right to its original position.

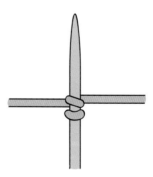

5. Bring the left strand under the needle, then up and over it from right to left. Bring the right strand under the needle, then up and over it from left to right.

6. Bring the left strand back over the needle, to the right of it, down, and under it.

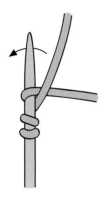

7. Bring the strand up to its original position.

8. Repeat steps 2–7 until you have one less stitch than needed. The slipknot counts as one stitch. The last loop in the next step will also count as one stitch.

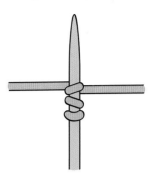

9. Bring the right strand to the left over the needle and down under it to make a final loop on the needle. Tie the two strands together under the needle to secure the stitches.

Begin double knitting as follows: *K1 through the back loop, slip 1 purlwise with yarn in front; repeat from *. Turn and repeat this row once, knitting the stitches normally. After a few rows of double knitting, switch to K1, P1 ribbing.

Provisional Cast Ons

The cast ons in this group are provisional in that they are used for a short time to enable you to start your work. Later, they are removed to expose live stitches that can be picked up and worked in different ways. For example, you might want to knit in the opposite direction so that both ends of your piece look exactly alike. Or you might want to graft two pieces together using the seamless Kitchener stitch, or add a decorative border. A provisional cast on can also be used to make a neat hem that is less bulky on the inside of a garment.

With most provisional cast ons, you will end up with one less stitch after removing the waste yarn. Increase one stitch on the first row after picking up the live stitches.

Choose a waste yarn about the same size as your project yarn. It should be strong so that it does not break when you pull it out. Using a waste yarn of a different color will help with removal of the cast on, as it will be easy to see. Using a smooth, slippery yarn is also helpful. Cotton is a good choice; embroidery floss can work well, but if it is too much smaller than your project yarn, the first row of stitches might be smaller than the rest. Avoid yarns that are fuzzy, as they can leave pesky fibers behind. In place of waste yarn, you might consider using ravel cord, a strong, slippery plastic cord popular among machine knitters.

Simple Provisional Cast On

Also called Two-Strand Provisional Cast On, Ribbon-Method Provisional Cast On, Ravel-Cord Cast On, Long-Tail Provisional Cast On, Invisible Cast On

This is simply the long-tail cast on using waste yarn. It's the most direct way of making a provisional cast on, but removing the waste yarn is extremely laborious.

1. Make a slipknot with the waste yarn and the project yarn together about 5" from the end of the strands and place the knot on the needle. Hold the needle in the right hand and the two strands taut in the left hand with the waste yarn in front of the working yarn. Insert the left thumb and index finger between the two strands, spread them apart, and twist them up to wrap the waste yarn around the left thumb and the working yarn around the left index finger.

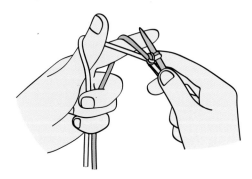

2. Cast on using the long-tail cast on: continental method (page 19) as follows: *insert the needle into the thumb loop from left to right as if to knit. Catch the front finger strand with the needle from the right and pull the strand back through the thumb loop. Remove the thumb from the loop, insert the thumb and index finger between the strands, and pull the tail toward you to tighten the stitch. Swing the thumb up to create a new thumb loop; repeat from *. (After the first stitch, you can switch to the long-tail cast on: English method on page 20 if you wish, wrapping the waste yarn around the thumb.) Do not count the slipknot as a stitch. Drop it after the first row.

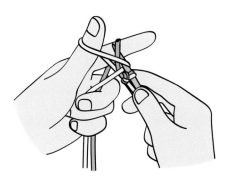

3. When you have finished casting on, break the waste yarn, leaving a 5" or 6" tail. With the project yarn, begin your project.
4. When ready for live stitches, carefully snip the waste yarn stitch by stitch, pick it out, and slip the live stitches onto a needle.

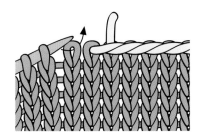

5. Increase one stitch in the first row.

Simple Provisional Cast On Variation

This variation requires both waste yarn and ravel cord. If you cannot find ravel cord, a very smooth yarn will also work.

1. With the waste yarn, cast on the required number of stitches using the long-tail cast on (page 18). Knit two or three rows of stockinette stitch and break the waste yarn.
2. Switch to the ravel cord and knit one row. Cut the ravel cord, leaving a 5" or 6" tail on both sides. Change to your project yarn and follow your pattern.

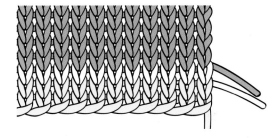

3. When ready for live stitches, carefully pull out the ravel cord. The waste yarn will be removed with the ravel cord. Pick up the live stitches.

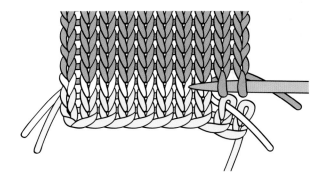

4. Increase one stitch in the first row.

Crocheted Provisional Cast On

Also called Crocheted Cast On, Provisional Crochet Cast On

This is the chain cast on using waste yarn. The waste yarn is much easier to remove in this method since you don't have to cut and pick it out. You will need a crochet hook.

1. With waste yarn, make a loose slipknot about 5" from the end and place it on the crochet hook. Hold the hook in your right hand and the needle in your left. Loop the working strand over the left index finger. *With the crochet hook above the needle and the working yarn below it, swing the hook from the left behind the strand on the index finger. Catch the yarn and pull the loop over the needle and through the slipknot. Bring the working yarn to the back under the needle.

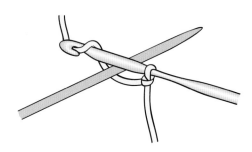

2. Repeat from * until you have one less than the required number of stitches. Slip the loop on the hook to the needle for the last stitch. Cut the waste yarn, leaving a 5" tail. Attach the project yarn and begin your project.

3. When ready for live stitches, start at the corner where there are two tails, one of waste yarn and one of project yarn. Pull the tail of project yarn through the end chain, and then pull the tail of waste yarn through the end chain and the first live stitch to free it. Pull the tail to unravel the crochet chain and pick up the live stitches.

Crochet Chain Provisional Cast On

Also called Japanese Crochet Cast On, Crochet Provisional Cast On, Vanishing Crochet Cast On

You will need a crochet hook a few sizes larger than the project needle, as well as waste yarn about the same weight as the project yarn. The crocheted chain is very easy to remove.

1. With waste yarn, make a slipknot about 5" from the end of the yarn and place it on the hook. Make a loose chain consisting of at least four chains more than the required number of stitches. Cut the waste yarn and elongate the last chain to keep the chain from unraveling.
2. Starting with the second chain from the end, use the project yarn and needles to pick up and knit one stitch through the back bump of each chain until you have the desired number of stitches. Continue your project.

3. When ready for live stitches, carefully pull the waste tail to unravel the chain, and pick up the live stitches.

Lifeline Provisional Cast On

This is a variation of the crochet chain provisional cast on. As the provisional edge is pulled out, it magically turns into a "lifeline" holding the live stitches. This technique requires a crochet hook and waste yarn.

1. With waste yarn, make a slipknot about 5" from the end of the yarn and place it on the hook. Make a loose chain consisting of half the number of chains as stitches to be cast on, plus several more. Cut the waste yarn and elongate the last chain to keep the chain from unraveling.

2. Starting a few chains from the end of the chain, use the project yarn and needle to *pick up and knit a stitch through the back bump of the chain. Bring the yarn to the front to make a yarn over. Repeat from * until the required number of stitches has been cast on, including the yarn overs. If working flat, cast on an extra stitch, ending with a pick up and knit. You can decrease the extra stitch later. Continue your project.

3. When ready for live stitches, carefully pull the waste tail to unravel the crochet chain.

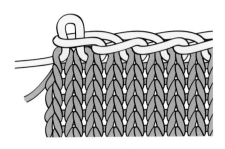

4. As the chain pulls out, it will turn into a single strand of waste yarn running through the live stitches. Transfer the stitches to a needle and continue with your project.

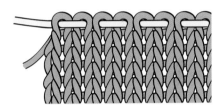

Open Chain Cast On

This cast on enables you to seamlessly add a knitted band to your work. It requires a crochet hook and waste yarn.

1. With waste yarn, make a slipknot about 5" from the end of the strand and place it on a crochet hook. Make a loose chain with four chains more than the required number of stitches. Cut the waste yarn and elongate the last chain to keep the chain from unraveling.
2. Starting with the second chain from the end, use the project yarn and needle to pick up and knit a stitch through the back bump of each chain until the required number of stitches has been picked up. Continue with your project.

3. When ready to work in the opposite direction or make the band, with the wrong side facing, use a smaller needle and the project yarn to pick up and knit through the isolated loops of the project yarn on the back behind the chain.

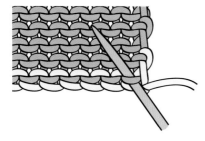

4. Work the stitches extending upward from the chain.

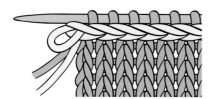

5. When finished working the band, carefully pull the waste tail to unravel the chain.

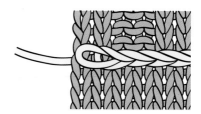

Provisional Wrap Cast On

Also called Invisible Cast On, Open Loop Cast On

This elastic edge is excellent for lace. The live stitches are slanting loops, so it is also ideal for whipping down if you are sewing a hem. It requires waste yarn.

1. Make a slipknot about 5" from the end of the yarn and place it on the needle. Make a slipknot in a piece of waste yarn and place it on the needle near the tip. Stretch the waste yarn along the underside of the needle and hold it in the left fingers.

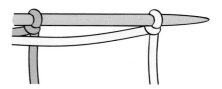

2. With the right hand, wrap the project yarn around the needle and the waste yarn, over the needle and away from you, under the needle and toward you. Make as many wraps over the needle as stitches required.

3. Holding the first stitch in position with the left index finger, drop the slipknot of waste yarn off the needle and wrap the end counterclockwise around the working strand. Knit the stitches on the first row through the back loop, and then continue knitting your project normally.

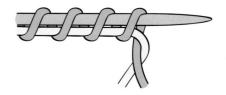

4. The live stitches are threaded on the waste yarn along the bottom edge.
5. When ready for live stitches, insert a needle into the stitches along the waste yarn and pull out the waste yarn.
6. Knit through the back loops on the first row.

Open Cast On

Also called Invisible Cast On, Invisible Provisional Cast On, Looping Provisional Cast On, Stranded Cast On

The open cast on is often confused with the tubular cast ons, probably because it is similar to the two-strand tubular cast on (page 82). It requires one needle two to three sizes larger than the project needle. You will also need waste yarn.

1. Cut a strand of waste yarn roughly four times longer than the width of the piece to be cast on. With the project yarn, make a slipknot about 5" from the end and place it on the needle. With the needle in the right hand, hold the end of the waste yarn in the right fingers with the slipknot tail. Wrap the waste yarn around the left thumb so that the strand is taut under the needle. Drape the working yarn over the left index finger.

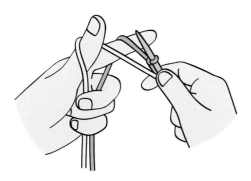

2. Bring the needle forward under the waste yarn and up between the two strands.

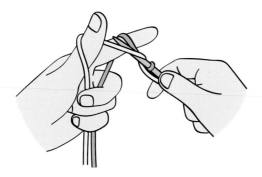

3. Bring the needle over the working yarn, down, and forward under both strands.

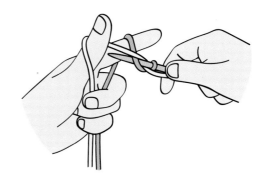

4. Bring the needle up to make a stitch.

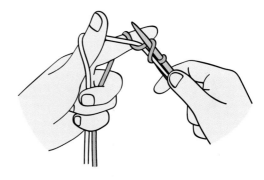

5. Swing the needle back over the working yarn, under it, and up between the two strands to form a second stitch.
6. Repeat steps 2–5 until you have the required number of stitches, trying to space them evenly to make them easier to work on the first row. Do not count the slipknot. Turn your work. Wrap the waste yarn counterclockwise around the working strand to secure the stitches and begin your project, dropping the slipknot after the first row. When ready for live stitches, gently pull out the waste yarn and pick up the stitches.

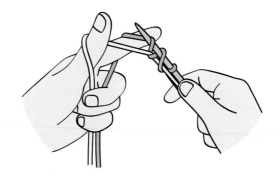

Open Cast On Variation

Use a circular needle instead of waste yarn. When you are ready for live stitches, just slip the needle onto the stitches and start knitting.

Special Cast Ons

This group encompasses a miscellaneous assortment of cast ons that are each helpful for a specific purpose—for example, when adding large numbers of stitches in the middle of a project, or when knitting a Möbius strip. Cast ons for socks, especially when knit from the toe up, fall into this category, but since there are so many of them, they have a section of their own.

Crochet Chain Cast On

This cast on can be used to add stitches at the end of a row or in the middle of a project, such as when knitting a garment from cuff to cuff. It requires a crochet hook one or two sizes larger than the needle.

Crochet chain cast on

1. Insert the hook into the edge stitch of the row below the last worked stitch on the needle, and pull through a loop of yarn from the working strand.

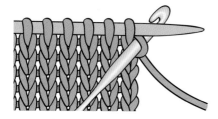

2. Starting with this loop, make a loose crocheted chain consisting of one less chain stitch than stitches to be cast on.

3. Transfer the loop from the hook to another needle, creating the first new stitch. Pick up and knit one stitch through the back bump of each chain, and then continue working across the row.

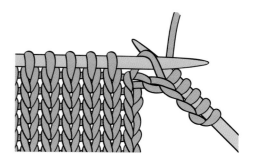

Buttonhole Cast On

Probably originally for buttonholes, this cast on is useful for steeks or when you need to add stitches in the middle of your work. Tightening the stitch can be difficult and takes practice.

Buttonhole cast on

1. Finish a right-side row. Do not turn your work.
2. With the needle in the right hand, hold the yarn taut in the left hand. *Swing the left thumb behind and under the strand, and then up to wrap the yarn

around the thumb. Insert the needle into the thumb loop as if to knit.

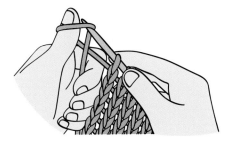

3. Wrap the yarn around the needle tip as if to knit, and lift the thumb loop up and over the needle tip and off the needle.

4. Place the left thumb on top of the stitch to keep it in position, and then tighten the stitch by pulling the yarn with the right fingers. Repeat from *.

Open Tube Cast On

This cast on enables you to make a seamless tube on two straight needles with double knitting. The edge will look like that of the backward-loop cast on.

Open tube cast on

1. With the needle in the right hand, hold the yarn taut between both hands, with the ball on the left and the tail in the right fingers. (You can also use a slipknot.) Swing the left thumb over, behind, and under the strand, and then up to create a loop around the thumb.

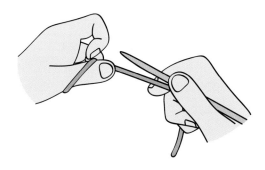

2. Insert the needle into the loop as if to knit, release the loop on the thumb, and pull the yarn to tighten the stitch. Repeat steps 1 and 2 to cast on half the number of stitches required. Turn.

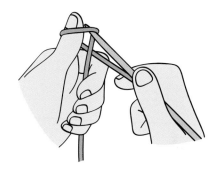

3. On the next row, with the working yarn in front at all times, *make a loop in the yarn and place it on the right needle, slip 1 purlwise with yarn in front; repeat from * to last stitch, slip 1 purlwise.

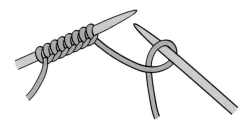

4. On all following rows, double knit as follows: *K1, slip 1 purlwise with yarn in front; repeat from *.

Double-Stitch Cast On

This variation of the long-tail cast on (page 18) enables you to make a seamless tube on two needles with double knitting. The edge on one side will look like that of the loop cast on (page 13); the other side will resemble the backward-loop cast on (page 14). Use two different colors if you would like to give each side a different appearance.

Double-stitch cast on, loop side

Double-stitch cast on, two-color version

1. Loosely tie together two strands of yarn about 5" from their ends. Hold the needle in the right hand with the knot under the needle. Pinch the knot with the right thumb and index finger to hold it in place. *Wrap one strand over the left index finger and the other around the left thumb.

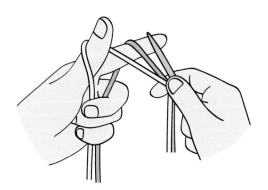

2. Insert the needle into the thumb loop as if to knit.

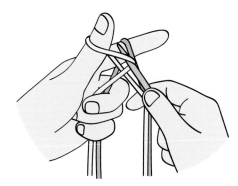

3. Swing the needle to the right over both index-finger strands, and then behind the far strand and up into the finger loop.

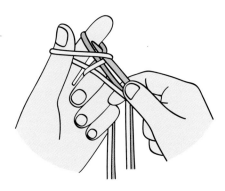

4. Remove both the thumb and index finger from their loops and pull the strands to tighten the stitches. Two stitches have been cast on. Repeat from * until you have cast on the required number of stitches.

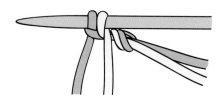

5. Begin double knitting: *K1, slip 1 purlwise with yarn in front; repeat from * for all rows.
   Work as follows if using two different colors (A and B).

   Row 1: With the color of the first stitch, *K1, slip 1 purlwise with yarn in front; repeat from *. Do not turn. Slide the stitches to the other end of the needle.

   Row 2: With the other color, *slip 1 purlwise with yarn in back, P1; repeat from *. Turn.

   Continue double knitting rows 1 and 2 on each side, one for each color, before turning. After several rows, untie the knot.

Emily Ocker's Circular Cast On

Also called Emily Ocker's Circular Beginning, Pinhole Cast On

Any circular piece that starts in the center, such as a shawl or afghan, will benefit from this cast on. Its heavy edge makes it less suitable for knitting socks from the toe up. Depending on the yarn you use, you may find it difficult to close the circle; sometimes the yarn sticks and knots up before the circle can be closed. Keeping the total number of stitches to a minimum will make the circle easier to close. A crochet hook and double-pointed needles are required.

Emily Ocker's circular cast on

1. Form a small circle with the yarn, with the working strand crossing over the tail. The tail will hang down and the working strand will be on the left.

2. Use the left thumb and fourth finger to hold the loop where the two strands cross, and keep the working strand taut between the left index and middle fingers. Insert the crochet hook into the circle and pull a loop of yarn through the circle.

3. Catch another loop of yarn without going through the circle, and pull the loop through the loop on the hook.

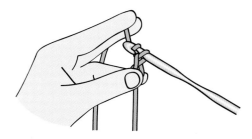

4. The tail and the circle will now be twisted together. Treat them both as one strand and repeat steps 2 and 3, picking up stitches around both strands until there are four stitches on the hook.

5. Transfer the stitches to a double-pointed needle. The loops should be tight enough so that the needle does not slip out. Make four more stitches as above and transfer them to another double-pointed needle. Repeat for a third needle.

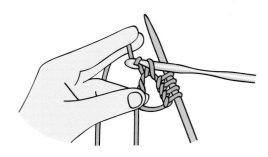

6. When you have cast on the required number of stitches, pull the tail to close the center hole as much as possible.

7. Knit the first round through the back loops if the stitches seem loose.

Circular Cast On

Also called Pinhole Cast On, Thom Christoph's Circular Beginning, Crochet Circular Cast On, Loop-de-Loop Cast On

The edge of this cast on is not quite as heavy as that created by Emily Ocker's circular cast on (page 95), so it is suitable for toe-up socks. A crochet hook can be used instead of a knitting needle.

Circular cast on

1. Make a loop in the yarn, crossing the working end over the tail. The tail will point down and the working end will extend up.

2. Use the left thumb and fourth finger to hold the loop where the two strands cross, and hold the working end taut between the left index and middle fingers.

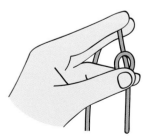

3. Insert the needle into the loop, catch the working strand from right to left, and pull it through the loop.

4. Catch the working strand from the right and above without going through the loop.

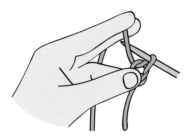

5. Repeat steps 3 and 4, moving the fingers holding the loop as you work around the circle. If casting on an even number of stitches, stop one short of the total stitches required.

6. Distribute the stitches evenly on double-pointed needles. If an even number of stitches is required, make a yarn over before joining and knitting the first round.

After working several rounds, pull the tail to close the hole.

Chain Circular Cast On

Also called Larger Hole Cast On, Easy-to-Start Cast On, Pinhole Cast On

You can use this method for any round or square project that starts in the middle. It requires a crochet hook in addition to needles. Double-pointed needles made of bamboo may prove best, as they are less likely to slip out as you cast on stitches on the second and third needles.

Chain circular cast on

1. Make a slipknot about 5" from the end of the yarn and place it on the hook. Make a single chain with one chain for each stitch to be cast on plus one extra. Make the chain into a circle by inserting the hook into the first chain and pulling a loop through the loop on the hook.

2. Insert the hook into the first chain and pull a loop through onto the hook.

3. Repeat step 2, inserting the hook into the next chain until there are four or five stitches on the hook, and transfer the stitches to a double-pointed needle.

4. Repeat steps 2 and 3 for the second and third needles until all chains have been used and the required number of stitches has been cast on. Continue your project.

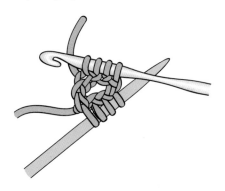

When the project is finished, thread the tail on a yarn needle and sew the edges of the chains together using an overcast stitch around the inside of the center hole. Pull tight and weave in the tail.

Lace Cast On

This variation of the cable cast on (page 51) forms a decorative, open edge that is quite flexible and well suited for lace projects. The loops along the edge also make it good for adding fringe. The edge tends to stretch, so the cast on is not suitable for pattern stitches that are too tight. The cast on creates an odd number of stitches. If your pattern requires an even number, cast on one extra stitch and untie the slipknot after working the first row.

Lace cast on

1. Make a slipknot about 5" from the end of the yarn and place it on the left needle. Place your left index finger on top of the knot to keep it in place. *With the right hand, wrap the working strand over the needle from back to front.

2. Insert the right needle under the left needle between the slipknot and the yarn over, wrap the yarn around the needle as if to knit, and pull it through.

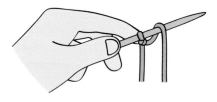

3. Place the needle tips together and slip the stitch from the right needle to the left. Repeat from *.

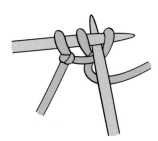

Iris Schreier's Möbius Cast On

This is the long-tail cast on: continental method adapted to making a true Möbius strip. It's a little more awkward than the next two Möbius cast ons, but with practice it flows quite easily. It requires a long circular needle with a very flexible cable.

Cast-on edge

Iris Schreier's Möbius cast on

1. Coil the cable once so that the needles are on either side of the coil. Hold the right needle and the cable in the right hand and let the left needle hang. Leaving a long tail, make a slipknot and place it on the right needle with the tail and the working strands in front of the cable.

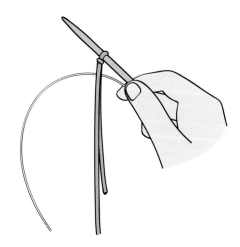

CAST ONS

2. With the left index finger, catch the working strand from behind and pull it under the cable to wrap it around the finger.

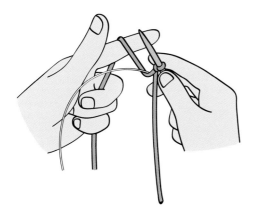

3. Insert the left thumb into the cable coil from the back and slip the cable over the thumb so that it lies between the thumb and the index finger. Wrap the tail around the thumb as for the long-tail cast on: continental method (page 19).

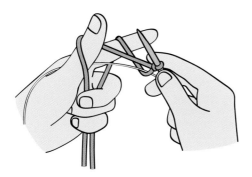

4. Insert the needle into the thumb loop as if to knit, swing the needle over the cable, catch the front finger strand with the needle from the right, and pull the strand back down through the thumb loop. Remove the thumb from the loop, insert it between the two strands, and pull the tail toward you to tighten the stitch.

5. Swing the thumb up to create a new loop.

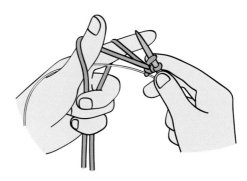

6. Bring the thumb with the strand wrapped around it under the cable to the back, and cast on one stitch by repeating steps 4 and 5.

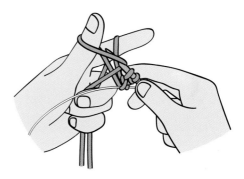

7. Bring the thumb and the strand wrapped around it back under the cable to the front, and repeat steps 4 and 5. Continue in this manner, alternating the thumb in front of or behind the cable until all stitches are cast on. Place a marker.

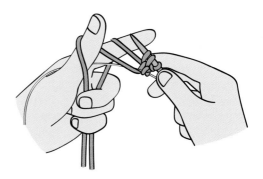

Knit the first stitch. Then knit the next and every alternate stitch through the back loop for the first half round (when the marker comes back to the top but is on the cable). Knit the remaining stitches normally, through the front loop. As you knit the first round, make sure you work the stitches in order. They have a tendency to cross over each other.

Cat Bordhi's Möbius Cast On

Here is another cast on that creates a true Möbius strip. It requires a long circular needle with a very flexible cable. You can see Cat demonstrating her cast on at http://www.youtube.com/watch?v=LVnTda7F2V4.

Cat Bordhi's Möbius cast on

Cast-on edge

1. Make a slipknot about 5" from the end of the yarn and place it on the needle. Slide the knot onto the cable part of the needle. Allow the right needle to hang down out of the way.

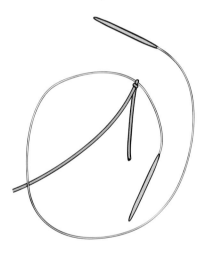

2. Pull the left needle around and hold it in your right hand. Pinch the slipknot with the right thumb and middle finger. (After casting on a few stitches, you can let the knot go.) Keep the working strand behind the needle and wrap it over the left index finger. Pinch the cable with the left thumb and middle finger.

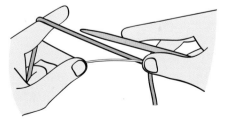

3. Swing the needle in front of the cable, under it, and up between the cable and the yarn.

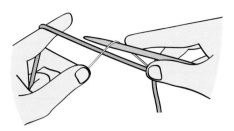

4. Swing the needle over the yarn and behind it.

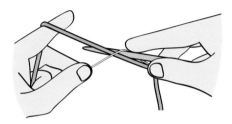

5. Bring the needle under the yarn, forward under the cable, and up.

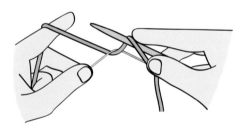

6. Swing the needle back over, behind, and under the yarn, and then forward and up. Repeat steps 3–6 until you have cast on the desired number of stitches, ending with step 5. Count only the stitches on the top needle.

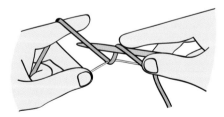

7. The needle will curl around forming a double loop as you cast on. Before knitting, make sure there is only one cross in the cable. Place a marker and knit the slipknot, and then knit across the stitches, knitting into every other stitch through the back loop on the first round only. Make sure you work the stitches in order. They have a tendency to cross over each other.

Rita Buchanan's Möbius Cast On

This is a relatively simple way of casting on to knit a true Möbius strip. You will need a long circular needle with a very flexible cable.

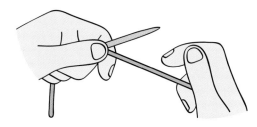

Rita Buchanan's Möbius cast on

1. With the needle in the left hand, hold the yarn taut between both hands with a short tail on the left and the ball on the right.

2. Swing the right thumb over, behind, and under the yarn, and then up to create a loop on the thumb.

3. Bend the thumb slightly away from you and insert the needle into the thumb loop as if to knit. Remove the thumb and pull the yarn to tighten the stitch. Repeat steps 2 and 3 to cast on the required number of stitches.

4. Slide all the stitches onto the cable part of the needle, and then rotate the row of stitches upward so that the cast-on edge is above the cable. Let the right needle hang.

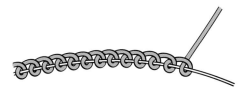

5. Starting with the last stitch cast on, use the left needle to pick up and purl the first stitch by inserting the needle between the first two stitches from back to front above the cable.

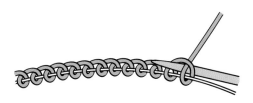

6. Continue to pick up and work stitches between the stitches above the cable, inserting the needle between the stitches from front to back for a knit stitch or from back to front for a purl stitch as your pattern requires. As you work around picking up stitches, make sure that the row of cast-on stitches is not twisted. The needle cable will automatically curl around on itself.

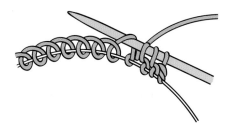

7. When you reach the tail end and can no longer pick up stitches, the needles should be pointing toward each other. Place a marker and begin your project.

Sock Cast Ons

If you are knitting the socks from the cuff down, you can use most of the cast ons in this book. Any cast on that gives you an elastic edge will work well. All except the rolled-edge cast ons in this group are for knitting socks from the toe up. Many originated between the Balkans and Afghanistan, where there is a rich tradition of sock knitting.

Rolled-Edge Cast On

This creates an elastic tubular edge on ribbing for socks knit from the cuff down. It requires waste yarn and ravel cord or a very smooth, strong yarn. It can be worked on double-pointed or circular needles.

Rolled-Edge Cast On for K1, P1 Rib

Rolled-edge cast on for K1, P1 rib

1. With waste yarn (shown in yellow), use any method to cast on half the number of required stitches. Join and work four rounds of stockinette stitch. Cut the waste yarn, leaving a 6" tail. Knit one round with the ravel cord (white). Cut the ravel cord, leaving a 6" tail.
2. With the project yarn, *K1, bring the yarn to front to create a yarn over; repeat from *. (If you are working on double-pointed needles, do not forget the yarn over when moving from one needle to the next.)

3. Work two rounds of double knitting:
   Round 1: *K1, slip 1 purlwise (the yarn over) with yarn in front; repeat from *.
   Round 2: *Slip 1 purlwise with yarn in back, P1; repeat from *.

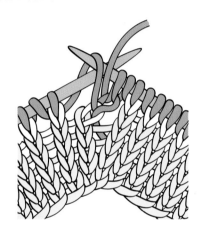

Begin K1, P1 ribbing. After working a few rounds, remove the smooth yarn or ravel cord by pulling the end. If you do not use ravel cord, you may need to pull out the yarn stitch by stitch, or snip it as you go along.

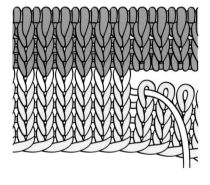

CAST ONS

Rolled-Edge Cast On for K2, P2 Rib

The number of stitches cast on must be a multiple of four.

Rolled-edge cast on for K2, P2 rib

1. Follow steps 1–3 for the rolled-edge cast on for K1, P1 rib (opposite). Cross two stitches as in steps 2 and 3 to create the K2, P2 ribbing.
2. *K1, drop the next (purl) stitch from the needle to the back of the work, K1.

3. Slip the dropped purl stitch back on the left needle and purl it, P1; repeat from *.

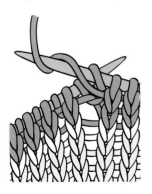

OR

2. **K1, bring the needle in front of the next purl stitch, and knit the next knit stitch, but leave it on the right needle.

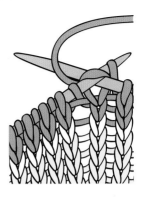

3. Bring the yarn to the front and purl the purl stitch, then drop both stitches from the left needle, P1; repeat from **.

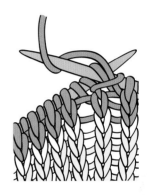

After repeating either rendition of steps 2 and 3 to cross stitches, continue in K2, P2 ribbing. Work several rounds, and then remove the smooth yarn or ravel cord.

Straight Wrap Cast On

Also called Turkish Cast On, Eastern European Cast On, Eastern Cast On, Mediterranean Cast On

Used in Turkish and Middle Eastern sock knitting, this cast on produces a seamless toe that is smooth inside. It can be used to start any round or closed project.

Straight wrap cast on

1. Hold two double-pointed needles parallel to each other in the left hand. Starting at the left and leaving at least a 5" tail, bring the working strand between the needles from front to back, and then forward over the top needle. (A slipknot can also be used on the top needle to start the wrap.) Wrap the yarn around both needles once for each stitch to be cast on. End by bringing the yarn behind the lower needle and forward between the two needles.

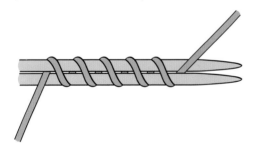

2. Slide the bottom needle to the right an inch or so to keep the bottom wraps from falling off as the top wraps are knit.

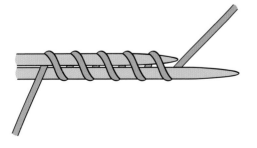

3. With the yarn in back, knit the stitches on the top needle.

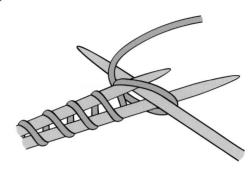

4. Being careful not to lose the last stitch knit, rotate the needles so that the bottom needle is on the top. Wrap the tail counterclockwise around the working strand to secure the last stitch.

5. Slide the bottom needle to the right about an inch and knit the stitches on the top needle. Distribute the stitches evenly on the needles and begin your pattern.

Straight Wrap Cast On Variation

This variation uses two circular needles.
1. Using two circular needles, wrap as in step 1 for the straight wrap cast on (above).
2. Pull the bottom needle to the right, sliding the wraps off the needle onto the cable portion. Let the needle hang. Using the other end of the top needle, knit the stitches on the needle.

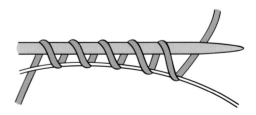

3. Rotate the needles and repeat step 2. Begin your pattern.

Figure-Eight Wrap Cast On

Wrapping the yarn in a figure eight around the needles makes a seamless, smooth toe.

Figure-eight wrap cast on

1. Hold two needles parallel to each other in the left hand. Starting at the left and leaving at least a 5" tail, *bring the yarn in front of the lower needle, between the two needles to the back, behind and over the top needle, between the two needles to the back, and under the bottom needle. Repeat from * until you have cast on the required number of stitches, counting the wraps on both needles and ending with the yarn coming over the bottom needle and between the two needles to the back. There is the same number of stitches on both needles.

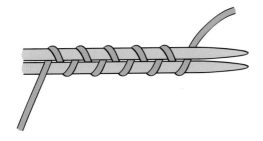

2. Slide the lower needle to the right an inch or so to keep the bottom stitches from falling off, and knit the stitches on the top needle.

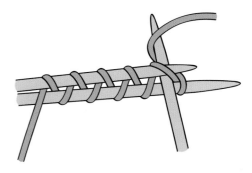

3. Being careful not to lose the last stitch knit, rotate the needles so that the bottom needle is on the top and the working strand is on the right. Wrap the tail counterclockwise around the working strand to secure the last stitch.

4. Slide the bottom needle to the right about an inch. With the yarn in back, knit the stitches on the top needle through the back loops. To create a firmer toe, you can knit the stitches through the front loops, but they will be twisted. Begin your project.

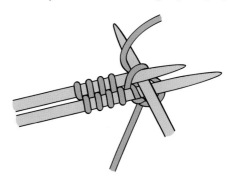

Backward-Loop Sock Cast On

Also called Patti's Quick Closed-Toe Cast On

This technique yields a smooth toe inside, with two rows of twisted stitches on the outside.

Backward-loop sock cast on

1. Hold two needles parallel to each other in the right hand along with the yarn tail. Hold the working end of the yarn in the left hand. *Swing the left index finger in front of the yarn, under it, and up to loop the strand over the finger.

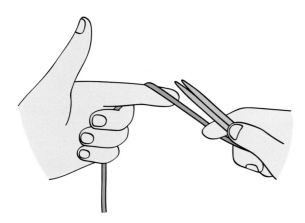

2. Crook the finger to create a loop on it. Insert one needle into the loop from left to right, remove the finger, and tighten the stitch.

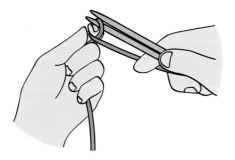

3. Make another loop on the index finger, transfer it to the other needle in the same way, and tighten the stitch. Repeat from *, alternating the needle on which the loop is placed until you have cast on the required number of stitches.

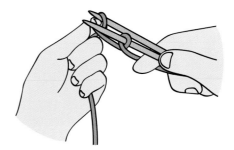

4. Rotate the needles so that the bottom needle is on the top and the working yarn is on the right. Using a third needle, knit the stitches on the top needle through the back loops.

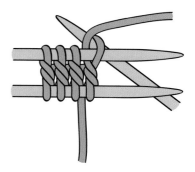

5. Rotate the needles and knit through the back loop of the stitches on the top needle.

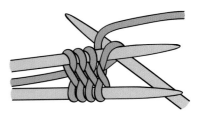

6. Rotate the needles and begin your project.

Judy's Magic Cast On

Also called Magic Cast On

This cast on from Judy Becker is similar to the backward-loop cast on. It is described here for a sock-knitting method using two circular needles, but you can also use double-pointed needles. Creating a seamless edge on both sides, this cast on is ideal for any small, closed circular beginning.

Judy's magic cast on

1. Hold the needles together pointing to the left. Leaving a long tail, make a slipknot and place it on the top needle. Insert the left thumb and index finger between the strands, spread them apart, and twist them up to wrap the tail around the index finger and the working strand around the thumb.

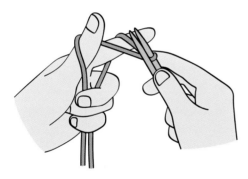

2. Bring the needles back over the finger strand, and then forward and up, slipping the strand between the needles to form a loop on the bottom needle.

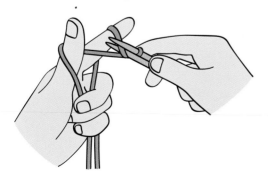

3. Bring the needles forward over the thumb strand, under it, back, and up, slipping the strand between the needles to form a loop on the top needle. Repeat steps 2 and 3 until you have the desired number of stitches, with the same number on each needle.

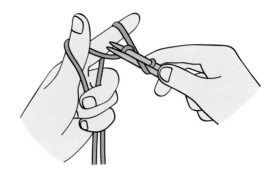

4. Rotate the needles so that the bottom needle is on the top and the working strand is on the right. Pull the bottom needle to the right, sliding the stitches onto the cable section. Pass the working strand over the tail and bring it to the back. Knit the stitches on the top needle using the other end of the top needle. If the first stitch is loose, pull the tail to tighten it.

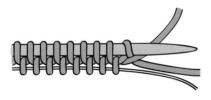

5. Rotate the needles so that the bottom needle is on the top. Push the top needle to the left, sliding the stitches back onto the top needle. Pull the bottom needle to the right, sliding the stitches onto the cable. With the other end of the top needle, knit the stitches on the top needle through the back loops. Begin your project.

Judy's Magic Cast On Variation

Use this variation when working two socks at the same time.

1. Work steps 1–3 of Judy's magic cast on (page 107) to cast on the first sock. Drop both the tail and the working strands and push the stitches to the back of the needles. With a new ball of yarn, works steps 1–3 to cast on the second sock.

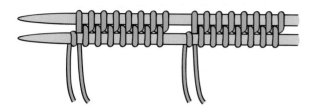

2. Rotate the needles and knit the stitches on the top needle for sock 1. Drop the yarn and repeat for sock 2. Then rotate the needles and knit stitches through the back loop on the top needle for sock 2, then for sock 1.

Closed-Toe Cast On

This cast on from Janet Rehfeldt creates a seamless toe with a slight ridge on the inside. Four double-pointed needles are required.

Closed-toe cast on

1. Cast on 10 stitches using the long-tail cast on (page 18).
2. Turn and rotate the work so the edge is above the needle.
3. Pick up and knit a stitch by inserting a second needle from front to back between the edge and second stitches on the bottom row just below the chain edge. Continue to pick up and knit stitches between the next two stitches until five stitches have been picked up. Using a third needle, pick up and knit five more stitches the same way. Work the last stitch through the end stitch on the first needle.

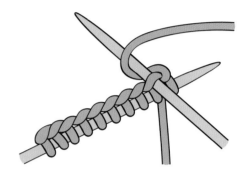

4. Rotate the work so that the first needle is back on the top. With the right side facing, knit the ten stitches on it. Then knit the five stitches on the next needle.

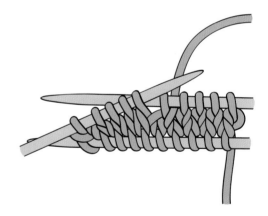

5. You are now at the center of the back of the foot and ready to begin your pattern.

The Best Toe-Up Cast On for Magic Loop

Kerrie James modified the closed-toe cast on (opposite) for the magic loop technique. A long circular needle is required. You can see Kerrie demonstrate this cast on at http://vimeo.com/4551095.

The best toe-up cast on for magic loop

1. With a circular needle, cast on 10 stitches using the long-tail cast on (page 18). Turn and slide the stitches onto the cable.

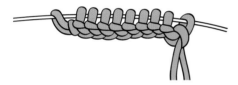

2. Pull the right needle (the one onto which you just cast stitches) out and around to create a loop. With the yarn in back and the wrong side facing, pick up and knit a stitch by inserting the right needle between the first two stitches from front to back.

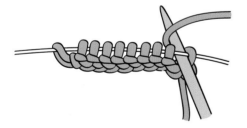

3. Holding the right needle in place and keeping the yarn in back, rotate the chain of cast-on stitches on the cable up so that the cast-on edge is above the cable.

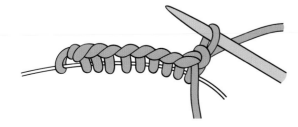

4. Bring the working strand to the back above the right needle tip. Pick up and knit another stitch by inserting the needle between the first two stitches above the cable again from front to back. Repeat this step, inserting the needle between the next two stitches across until there are 10 stitches on both the top needle and the cable.

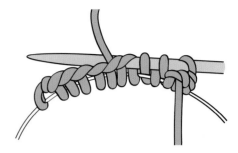

5. Rotate the work clockwise so that the stitches on the cable are on the top. Push the top needle to the left to bring the stitches back onto the needle. Pull the lower needle out and around to make a loop and use it to knit the stitches on the needle.

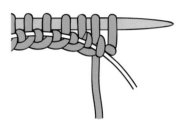

6. Rotate the work again so that the stitches on the cables are on the top, push the top needle to the left to bring the stitches back onto the needle, and then pull the lower needle out and around to make a loop. Knit one or two stitches to where the tail is. Bring the tail between the needles to the back and finish the row.

7. Start working in the round using the magic loop technique.

Sock Cast Ons

CAST ONS

109

Easy Toe Cast On

Wendy Johnson utilizes the crochet chain provisional cast on (page 88) to create a smooth, seamless toe. It requires waste yarn and a crochet hook.

Easy toe cast on

1. With a piece of waste yarn and a crochet hook, make a loose chain with three or four more chains than the number of stitches required. Break the yarn, loosely pull the tail through the last chain just enough to secure the chain, and tie a knot in its end.
2. With the project yarn and a double-pointed needle, pick up and knit a stitch through the back bump of each chain until you have the required number of stitches.

3. Work four rows of stockinette stitch.
4. Rotate the needle so that the cast-on edge is on top. The tail with the knot will be on the left.

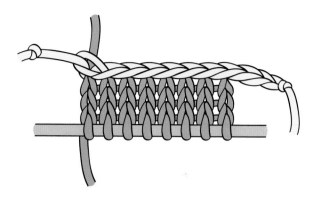

5. Undo the knot end of the chain by pulling the tail back through the last chain, and gently pull the tail to unravel the chain and pick up the live stitches. The two needles will be parallel to each other with the same number of stitches on each. Begin your project.

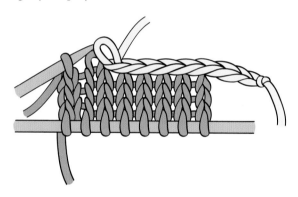

Patti's Closed-Toe Crochet Chain Cast On

This cast on from Patti Pierce Stone creates a firm, durable toe that is smooth on the inside. It uses a crochet hook as well as needles. Either double-pointed or circular needles can be used.

Patti's closed-toe crochet chain cast on

1. With a crochet hook, chain seven.
2. Turn the chain so that it is horizontal and the tail is on the left. Starting with the second chain, insert the hook into the center of the chain to pick up a stitch through each of the next five chains.

3. Transfer the six stitches on the hook to a needle. Rotate the chain so that the stitches on the needle are on the bottom and the top loops of the chains are on the top.

4. Starting with the second chain, again insert the hook under the lower side of the chain and into the center of the chain to pick up a stitch through each of the next six chains.

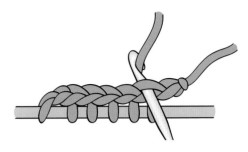

5. Transfer these stitches to another needle. Rotate the work and begin working in the round. The tail of the chain with the extra stitch on it will be on the inside of the toe. After finishing your sock, undo the knot, pull out the extra stitch, and weave the end in.

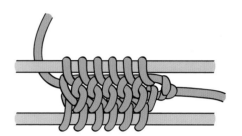

It All Ends with Binding Off

Once you've finished knitting, you need to remove the stitches from the needles and secure them so that your hard work does not unravel. This is called binding off, or sometimes casting off.

As with casting on, there are many ways to bind off. Each technique produces an edge with distinctive characteristics. Some are firm and rigid while others are elastic. Many create a decorative edge that can be incorporated into the design of your project. Binding off can also be used during the knitting process to help shape an element, such as armholes and necklines, or to make buttonholes. Many of the bind offs in this book offer versatility that makes them appropriate for most projects; a few have more specialized uses.

It's important that the elasticity of the bound-off edge be in keeping with the fabric you have made and its function. If it's too tight and firm, the edge will pull in, causing the upper portion of your work to pucker. If the edge is too loose and flexible, it will flare out and ripple.

Many bind offs have corresponding cast ons. You can use these pairings to give your bottom and top edges a matching appearance.

After binding off, you are left with one stitch on the right needle. Unless otherwise stated, secure this last stitch by breaking the yarn and pulling the tail through the last loop.

Tips for Binding Off

If you bind off in pattern—that is, you maintain your pattern when working the stitches as you bind them off—you will generally find that the bound-off edge of your work will better maintain its tension and appearance. If the bound-off edge will be sewn to another piece, the seam is also less likely to be noticeable if it's in the pattern. If you're knitting lace and the pattern calls for a yarn over, put in the yarn over before binding off to keep the edge from being too tight. If you have cables in your piece, work the crossover in the bind-off row to keep the edge from splaying, or knit two stitches together along the top of the cable.

Often the last stitch to be bound off is elongated and floppy. This is not a problem if the edge will be hidden in a seam, but if the edge will be visible, a neater stitch is desirable. In this situation, bind off all but the last stitch. There will be one stitch on each needle. Slip the stitch on the left needle to the right needle. With the left needle, pick up the side of the edge stitch in the previous row immediately below the slipped stitch. Transfer the slipped stitch back to the left needle, knit the two stitches together, and then finish binding off.

Another way of preventing this enlarged stitch involves two rows of work. On the row before binding off, slip the first stitch as if to purl, and then finish the row. Bind off normally on the next row.

When binding off in circular knitting, there will be a break in the edge between the first and last stitches bound off. You can make the edge look continuous by binding off all stitches except the last one. Pull this stitch so that it is 5" or 6" long, and then cut it at the top of the loop and pull out the end attached to the ball. Thread the strand onto a yarn needle and insert the needle under the two side strands of the first bound-off stitch. Then insert the needle into the center of the last bound-off stitch and pull the yarn through to create a new stitch, matching the tension of the rest of the bound-off stitches. Then weave the end in on the back of your work.

Chain Bind Offs

This is a large group of bind offs that produce a chain along the edge. The chain isn't always exactly on top of the edge, however. Sometimes it lies slightly to the front or the back. On some, such as the standard bind off, you can make the chain lean to one side or the other, turning the placement of the chain into a design element.

Some knitters have difficulty controlling the tension on chain bind offs because they involve lifting one stitch over another and off the needle. If you are not careful, the stitches can become elongated, resulting in a chain that is not neat and even. Practice to get the tension right, or try a different style of bind off that does not involve lifting one stitch over another.

Some of these bind offs are more elastic than others, while some lengthen the edge in a way that works well with patterns producing scalloped, wavy, or heavily pointed edges.

Without Knitting Bind Off

Also called Binding Off Without Yarn, Slip-Stitch Bind Off

This is a simple bind off that does not require any more yarn once you have finished knitting. The edge is very tight and not stretchy, making it particularly good for buttonholes.

Without knitting bind off

1. Slip two stitches from the left needle to the right as if to knit. With the left needle, lift the right stitch on the right needle over the left and off the needle.
2. Slip one stitch from the left needle to the right as if to knit, and lift the right stitch over the left stitch and off the needle. Repeat this step. Using a tapestry needle and a piece of yarn, sew the last stitch to the edge of the piece.

Standard Bind Off

Also called Basic Bind Off, Plain Bind Off, Chain Bind Off, Lift-Over Bind Off, Pullover Cast Off, Traditional Bind Off

This is probably the most commonly used bind off, and for many knitters it's the only one they use. It creates a neat edge that is firm yet elastic and is appropriate for most uses. It is a good bind off to be familiar with, as many bind offs and some cast ons utilize it. Pair it with the chain cast on (page 63) for matching edges.

This bind off can be performed in several ways, each affecting the final look of the edge. If you knit all the stitches as you bind them off, the edge will roll forward. If you purl all the stitches, the edge will roll back. If you alternate knit and purl stitches, the edge will be straight with the chain along the top.

If you have trouble maintaining an even tension, use a right-hand needle one to two sizes larger than the project needle. Also try not to stretch the stitch as you lift it.

Standard bind off, chain rolling forward

Standard bind off, chain rolling back

Standard bind off, chain on top

1. K2, and with the left needle lift the right stitch on the right needle over the left stitch and off the needle.

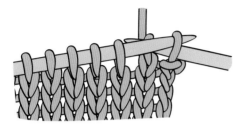

2. K1, and lift the right stitch over the left stitch and off the needle. Repeat this step. On a purl row, bring the yarn to the back before lifting the stitch over and off the needle.

Standard Bind Off: Twice-Worked Variation

Also called Twice-Worked Bind Off

The extra knit stitch makes the edge a little more open than that of the standard bind off (above). It also has a tendency to spread and ruffle a bit. Using a smaller needle helps to prevent spreading.

1. *K2. With the left needle, lift the right stitch over the left and off the needle.
2. Slip the stitch just made back to the left needle. Repeat from *.

Crochet Bind Off

Also called Crocheted Bind Off, Single-Crochet Bind Off

This variation of the standard bind off (page 114) uses a crochet hook instead of a second needle. It is good for cotton, linen, and silk, as it is easier to control the size of the stitches. It also works well with irregular or novelty yarns. The hook should be about the same size as your needle.

Crochet bind off

1. Insert the hook into the first stitch as if to knit, catch the working strand, and pull a loop through, dropping the stitch from the left needle.

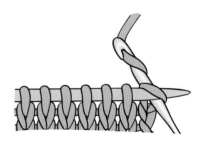

2. Insert the hook into the next stitch as if to knit, and catch the working yarn.
3. Pull a loop through both the stitch on the needle and the stitch on the hook. Drop the stitch from the left needle.

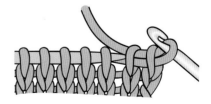

4. Repeat steps 2 and 3 until all stitches are bound off. Keep the loop on the hook fairly loose. On a purl row, bring the yarn to the front of your work and insert the hook into the first stitch as if to purl, then work as above, purling instead of knitting.

Chain Bind Offs   115

Double-Crochet Bind Off

Also called Single-Crochet Bind Off

This variation of the crochet bind off (page 115) adds an additional wrap for each stitch. While this makes the edge quite elastic, it also makes it spread. The crochet hook should be about the same size as the project needles. However, if the edge spreads out too much, counteract the problem by trying a smaller hook.

Double-crochet bind off

1. Insert the hook into the first stitch as if to knit, catch the working strand, and pull a loop through, dropping the stitch from the needle. *Repeat this step once. There are now two loops on the hook.

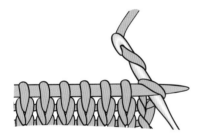

2. Wrap the yarn around the hook as if to knit, and pull the yarn through both loops on the hook. Repeat from *.

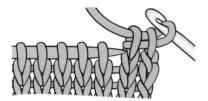

Braided-Rib Bind Off

This variation of the standard bind off (page 114) creates a thick edge that is durable and decorative but not very elastic.

Braided-rib bind off

1. Hold a second strand of yarn next to the working strand, leaving about a 5" tail on the new strand. Use both together as the working strand.

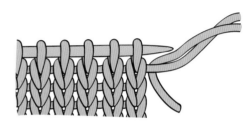

2. Purl two stitches to make two double stitches.
3. With the left needle, lift the right double stitch over the left and off the needle. *P1, lift the right double stitch over the left and off the needle. Repeat from *.

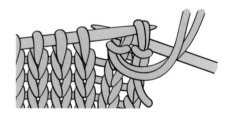

Chain Bind Offs

BIND OFFS

One-Over-Two Bind Off

Also called Decrease Bind Off

This variation of the standard bind off (page 114) produces a tight edge that is particularly good with an allover cable pattern because it prevents the top of the cables from spreading. It is also effective for tubular and double knitting.

One-over-two bind off

1. K3, and with the left needle lift the right stitch on the right needle over the other two stitches and off the needle.

2. K1, and lift the right stitch over the other two stitches and off the needle. Repeat this step until two stitches remain on the right needle. Lift the right stitch over the left and off the needle.

Double-Stitch Bind Off

This variation of the one-over-two bind off (at left) uses two colors to create a decorative but tight edge.

Double-stitch bind off

1. On the last row before binding off, work two alternating colors.

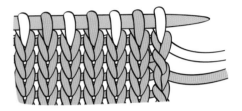

2. On the bind-off row, loosely K3 in the color sequence established. With the left needle, lift the right stitch on the right needle over the other two stitches and off the needle.

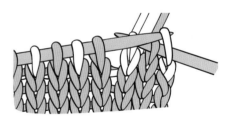

3. Maintaining the color sequence, K1, and lift the right stitch over the other two stitches and off the needle. Repeat this step.

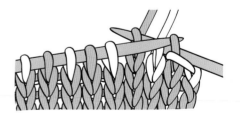

BIND OFFS

Ribbing Bind Off

Also called One-Row Flat-Chain Bind Off

This variation of the standard bind off (page 114) produces an edge that looks just like the standard bind-off edge, but it is slightly stretchier. It is suitable for any ribbing.

Ribbing bind off

1. P2tog, K1. With the left needle, lift the right stitch on the right needle over the left stitch and off the needle.
2. Bring the yarn to the front and slip the stitch purlwise from the right needle to the left.

3. Repeat steps 1 and 2, ending P2tog.

Ribbing Bind Off: K2, P2 Variation

Ribbing bind off: K2, P2 variation

1. K2, and with the left needle lift the right stitch on the right needle over the left stitch and off the needle.

2. Bring the yarn to the front and slip the stitch just made purlwise to the left needle.

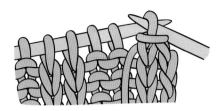

3. P2tog and slip the stitch just made purlwise to the left needle. P2tog.
4. Bring the yarn to the back and K1, and then with the left needle lift the right stitch on the right needle over the left and off the needle.
5. K1, and with the left needle lift the right stitch on the right needle over the left and off the needle.
6. Repeat steps 2–5, ending with step 3.

Cable Bind Off

This variation of the ribbing bind off (at left) is good for both seed stitch and K1, P1 ribbing. If the edge flares out, use a needle one or two sizes smaller than the project needle.

Cable Bind Off for Seed Stitch

Cable bind off for seed stitch

1. If the first stitch on the left needle is a purl: K1, *bring the yarn to the front. Slip the stitch on the right needle purlwise to the left needle.

2. P2tog, move the yarn to back and slip the stitch on the right needle purlwise to the left needle, K2tog.

3. Repeat from *. If the first stitch on the left needle is a knit stitch: P1, slip the stitch to the left needle with the yarn in back, K2tog. Repeat from *.

Cable Bind Off for K1, P1 Rib

Cable bind off for K1, P1 rib

1. If the first stitch on the left needle is a purl: P1, *with the yarn in back, slip the stitch on the right needle purlwise to the left needle.

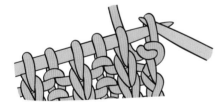

2. K2tog, move the yarn to front, and then slip the stitch back onto the right needle to the left needle, P2tog.

3. Repeat from *. If the first stitch on the left needle is a knit: K1, slip the stitch to the left needle with the yarn in front, P2tog. Repeat from *.

Russian Bind Off

A variation of the standard bind off (page 114), this method is actually worked in a way similar to the Icelandic bind off (page 124). The extra wrap creates a stretchy edge.

Russian bind off

1. K1, *slip the stitch from the right needle purlwise to the left.
2. Insert the right needle into the slipped stitch on the left needle as if to purl, and then insert it into the second stitch as if to knit.

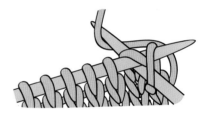

3. Wrap the yarn around the right needle and pull the new loop through both stitches on the left needle, dropping both from the left needle. Repeat from *.

Suspended Bind Off

Also called Elastic Bind Off

This bind off produces an edge that is slightly more elastic than that of the standard bind off because the bound-off stitch is elongated.

Suspended bind off

1. Slip one stitch as if to purl, K1, *with the left needle lift the right stitch on the right needle over the left stitch but leave it on the left needle.

2. Knit the next (second) stitch, then slip both the just-worked stitch and the lifted stitch off the left needle. Two stitches are on the right needle.

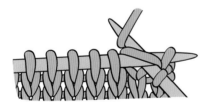

3. Repeat from * until two stitches remain, lift the first stitch on the right needle over the second and off the needle.

Suspended Bind Off Variation

This creates an even, stretchy edge.

1. K2, but do not drop the second stitch from the left needle.

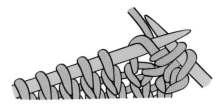

2. With the left needle, lift the right stitch on the right needle over the left stitch and off the needle. Then drop the rest of the second stitch from the left needle.

3. *K1, but do not drop the stitch from the left needle.

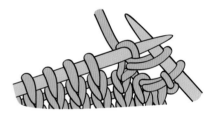

4. With the left needle, lift the right stitch on the right needle over the left stitch and off the needle. Then drop the rest of the second stitch from the left needle.

5. Repeat from * until the last stitch, K1, and lift the right stitch over the left.

Stretchy Bind Off

This bind off, attributed to Sarah Hauschka, creates an elastic edge for K1, P1 ribbing by working each stitch twice. It creates a neat chain across the top edge, making it good for cuffs, hems, and neckbands.

Stretchy bind off

1. K1, but leave the stitch on the left needle. Bring the yarn to the front.

2. P2tog (the second stitch that remained on the left needle and the one next to it), drop the first stitch of the two just purled together (the one closest to the needle tip) off the left needle, but keep the second stitch on it.

3. With the left needle, lift the right stitch on the right needle over the left stitch and off the needle. Bring the yarn to the back. The first stitch is still on the left needle.

4. K2tog (the first stitch that remained on the left needle and the one next to it).

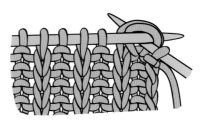

5. Drop the first of the two stitches just knit together (the one closest to the needle tip) off the left needle, but keep the second stitch on the needle.

6. With the left needle, lift the right stitch on the right needle over the left and off the needle. Bring the yarn to the front.

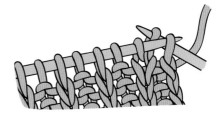

7. Repeat steps 2–6.

Two-Row Bind Off
for K1, P1 Rib

This method creates a large flat chain along the edge. It is good for ribbing and tubular fabrics. The edge tends to be tight, so work it loosely or on larger needles if you want a stretchier edge.

Two-row bind off for K1, P1 rib

1. *K1, P1, with the left needle lift the second stitch in from the tip on the right needle over the stitch closest to the tip and off the needle. Repeat from * across the row. Half the stitches have been bound off. Break the yarn.

2. Turn the work. Slip two stitches from the left needle to the right as if to purl, and with the left needle lift the right stitch on the right needle over the left stitch and off the needle.

3. Slip one stitch from the left needle to the right as if to purl, and lift the right stitch on the right needle over the left stitch and off the needle. Repeat this step across the row until one stitch remains. Using a tapestry needle and a piece of yarn, sew the last stitch to the edge of the piece.

Two-Row Bind Off
for K2, P2 Rib

This edge is not quite as open as the two-row bind off for K1, P1 rib above.

Two-row bind off for K2, P2 rib

1. K2, with the left needle lift the second stitch in from the tip on the right needle over the stitch closest to the tip and off the needle.

2. P2, with the left needle lift the second stitch in from the tip on the right needle over the stitch closest to the tip and off the needle.
   Repeat steps 1 and 2 across the row. Half the stitches have been bound off. Break the yarn.

3. Turn the work. Slip two stitches from the left needle to the right as if to purl. With the left needle, lift the right stitch on the right needle over the left stitch and off the needle.

4. Slip one stitch from the left needle to the right as if to purl, and lift the right stitch on the right needle over the left stitch and off the needle. Repeat this step until one stitch remains. Using a tapestry needle and a piece of yarn, sew the last stitch to the edge of the piece.

Decrease Bind Off

Also called K2tog Bind Off, Alternate Bind Off, Russian Bind Off, Lace Bind Off, English Bind Off, Twice-Worked Bind Off, Twisted Bind Off, Stretchy Bind Off, TL Stretchy Bind Off

Because this bind off does not involve lifting stitches over others, it's easier to control the tension. The edge is slightly more elastic than the standard bind-off edge, making this a useful option for sock cuffs and neckbands.

Decrease bind off

*K2tog through the back loops and slip the just-knit stitch back onto the left needle; repeat from *.

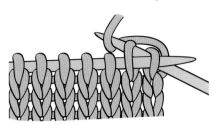

Decrease Bind Off: Russian Variation

This version is worked on the purl side.

P1, *slip the stitch back to the left needle, P2tog; repeat from *.

Elastic Bind Off

Also called TL Stretchy Bind Off

This variation of the decrease bind off (at left) adds a second wrap to give more length to the edge, making it quite stretchy. It is particularly good with K1, P1 ribbing or seed stitch.

Elastic bind off

K2, *insert the left needle into the front of both stitches on the right needle from left to right and knit the two stitches together through the back loops, K1; repeat from *.

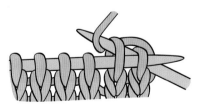

Decorative Bind Offs

These bind-off techniques are especially distinctive for their decorative appeal, although many have a tendency to stretch the edge. Some have corresponding cast ons, enabling you to create the same edge on both ends of your work.

K2tog Bind Off

Also called Knit Two Together Bind Off

Although similar in execution to the decrease bind off (page 123), this creates a firm edge that looks very different. It is good for binding off in the middle of a row, especially for a buttonhole.

K2tog bind off

*K2tog, and slip the stitch on the right needle to the left needle. Repeat from *.

Icelandic Bind Off

Also called Stretchy Bind Off

This variation of the decrease bind off (page 123) creates an edge with a braided appearance.

Icelandic bind off

1. With the yarn in back, insert the tip of the right needle into the first stitch on the left needle as if to purl and catch the right side of the second stitch.

2. Pull the second stitch through the first stitch and knit it, slipping both stitches off the needle.

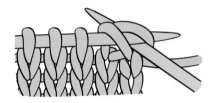

3. Slip the stitch from the right needle to the left.
4. Repeat steps 1–3.

Simple Two-Color Bind Off

This variation of the standard bind off (page 114) enables you to carry a color sequence up through the bound-off edge—for example, with corrugated ribbing. It also works well with a two-color brioche stitch. Colors are designated as A and B.

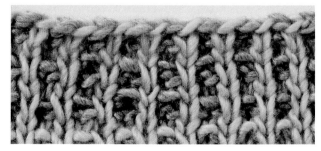

Simple two-color bind off

1. Work an A stitch with B, and then work a B stitch with A.

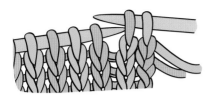

2. With the left needle, lift the right stitch on the right needle over the left stitch and off the needle.

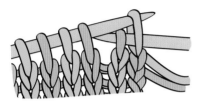

3. Work the next stitch with the alternate color. With the left needle, lift the right stitch on the right needle over the left stitch and off the needle. Repeat this step.

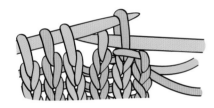

I-Cord Bind Off

Also called Applied I-Cord, Two-Stitch or Three-Stitch I-Cord Bind Off, Corded Bind Off

This bind off creates a neat, decorative I-cord edge. It makes an appealing design element along necklines, seams, and the tops of pockets, especially when done in a contrasting color. If you take this approach, work the last row of your knitting in the contrasting color to make a clear delineation with the main color.

You can change the size of the I-cord by casting on more or fewer stitches. Always knit together the last I-cord stitch and the first stitch to be bound off. Pair this with the I-cord cast on (page 65) for matching edges.

I-cord bind off

1. Cast on three stitches using the knit cast on (page 48) as follows: *knit the first stitch, but leave the stitch on the left needle. Rotate the right needle clockwise, insert the tip of the left needle into the stitch from left to right, and remove the right needle; repeat from * twice more. These three stitches are the I-cord stitches.

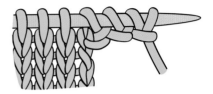

2. K2, K2tog through the back loops. You are knitting together the last I-cord stitch and the first stitch to be bound off.

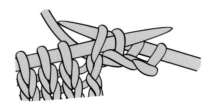

3. Place the needle tips together, slip the three stitches from the right needle to the left, and pull the yarn tight.

   Repeat steps 2 and 3 until only the three I-cord stitches remain on the left needle.

4. K2, with the left needle lift the right stitch on the right needle over the left stitch and off the needle, K1, lift the right stitch over the left stitch and off the needle.

Edging Bind Off

Also called Border Bind Off

Add a decorative border to the edge while binding off. A cable was used here, but you can choose any border you want, such as a strip of lace or a fancy rib. The number of stitches required for the border will determine the number of stitches you need to cast on in step 1. For an added bonus, pair this with the edging cast on (page 66) for matching edges.

Edging bind off

1. Cast on the edging stitches using the knit cast on (page 48) as follows: *knit the first stitch, but leave the stitch on the left needle. Rotate the right needle clockwise, insert the tip of the left needle into the stitch from left to right, and remove the right needle. Repeat from * until you have cast on to the needle however many stitches are needed for the edging.

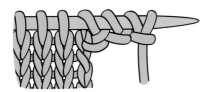

2. Work all but the last edging stitch in pattern. Depending on your pattern, K2tog or P2tog, working together the last edging stitch and the first stitch to be bound off. For some patterns, K2tog through the back loops may work better than K2tog. Turn and work the edging stitches in pattern. Turn. Continue to repeat this step. The number of edging stitches will always remain the same while the rest of the stitches will decrease.

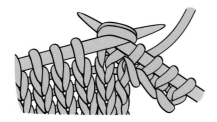

3. When only the edging stitches remain, turn work and bind them off using the standard bind off (page 114) as follows: work two stitches, lift the right stitch over the left stitch and off the needle, *work the next stitch, lift the right stitch over the left stitch and off the needle; repeat from *.

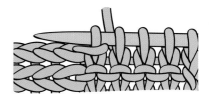

Picot Bind Off 1

This bind off creates an open, slightly ruffled edge decorated with picot points. You can vary the frequency and spacing of the points by binding off more or fewer stitches between casting on. These bind offs can be paired with the picot cast ons (page 69) for matching edges.

Picot bind off 1

1. Bind off two stitches using the standard bind off (page 114) as follows: K2, with the left needle lift the right stitch on the right needle over the left stitch and off the needle, K1, lift the right stitch over the left and off the needle. Turn the work.

2. With the wrong side facing, cast on three stitches using the knit cast on (page 48) as follows: *knit the first stitch on the left needle, but leave the stitch on the needle. Rotate the right needle clockwise, insert the tip of the left needle into the stitch from left to right, and remove the right needle; repeat from * twice.

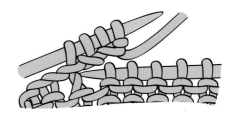

3. Turn the work and bring the yarn to the back. Counting from the left, lift the second (illustrated below), third, and fourth stitches on the right needle one by one over the first stitch and off the needle. One stitch remains on the right needle. Slip the stitch from the right needle to the left.

4. Repeat steps 1–3.

Picot Bind Off 2

This bind off is worked on the wrong side, creating thick picot points that have a tendency to roll forward. Working loosely makes it easier to do.

Picot bind off 2

1. With the wrong side facing, bind off three stitches using the standard bind off (page 114), purling as follows: P2, with the yarn in back lift the right stitch on the right needle over the left stitch and off the needle, *P1, lift the right stitch over the left and off the needle; repeat from * once. With the yarn in front, slip the stitch on the right needle to the left needle.

2. P2tog loosely and bring the yarn to the back.
3. Insert the right needle between the first two stitches on the left needle from back to front.

4. Bring the yarn to the front, wrap the yarn around the right needle as if to purl to create a yarn over, and pull the stitch through to the back, but do not drop the first stitch off the left needle.

5. With the yarn in front, slip the just-made stitch (not the yarn over) back to the left needle, bring the yarn to the back to make another yarn over, and purl the just-made stitch.

6. Slip all four stitches from the right needle to the left.
7. P2tog, and with the yarn in front slip the stitch on the right needle to the left. Repeat this step four more times, ending by keeping the stitch on the right needle. Bring the yarn to the back.
8. Repeat steps 3–7.

Picot Point Bind Off 1

Also called Picot Bind Off

This is one bind off where working tightly is an advantage because it helps define the points, but you won't sacrifice elasticity. You can make the points with any number of stitches as long as you bind off twice the number of stitches that you cast on. Two stitches can yield a very subtle effect, while four or six stitches will produce very pronounced points.

Picot point bind off 1 made casting on two stitches

1. Cast on two (or four or six) stitches using the knit cast on (page 48) as follows: *knit the first stitch, but leave the stitch on the left needle. Rotate the right needle clockwise, insert the tip of the left needle into the stitch from left to right, and remove the right needle; repeat from * once more.
2. K2, with the left needle lift the right stitch on the right needle over the left stitch and off the needle, *K1, lift the right stitch over the left and off the needle; repeat from * three more times, binding off a total of two stitches. Slip the remaining stitch back onto the left needle.

3. Repeat steps 1 and 2.

Picot Point Bind Off 2

Worked on the wrong side, this bind off creates more subtle picot points.

Picot point bind off 2

1. With the wrong side facing, cast on two stitches using the knit cast on (page 48) as follows: *knit the first stitch, but leave the stitch on the left needle. Rotate the right needle clockwise, insert the tip of the left needle into the stitch from left to right, and remove the right needle; repeat from * once more.
2. With the right needle, lift the second stitch in from the tip of the left needle over the stitch closest to the tip and off the needle, then lift the now-second stitch in from the tip over the one closest to the tip and off the needle.

3. Slip the first stitch to the right needle as if to purl, K1, lift the right stitch on the right needle over the left and off the needle.

4. Slip the stitch on the right needle to the left needle.
5. Repeat steps 1–4.

Crown Picot Bind Off

In this method, a number of picot points are joined to form half circles, or crowns, along the edge. You can make the crowns smaller or larger by changing the number of picot points in each one. You can also alter the spacing between the crowns by changing the number of bound-off stitches between them.

Crown picot bind off

1. Cast on two stitches using the knit cast on (page 48) as follows: *knit the first stitch, but leave the stitch on the left needle. Rotate the right needle clockwise, insert the tip of the left needle into the stitch from left to right, and remove the right needle; repeat from * once more.
2. K2, with the left needle lift the right stitch on the right needle over the left stitch and off the needle, K1, lift the right stitch over the left and off the needle.

3. Slip the stitch from the right needle to the left. This makes one picot point. Repeat steps 1–3 three times to make three more points, or as many as you wish for the crown.

4. Bind off four stitches, or however many you want between the crowns, using the standard bind off (page 114) as follows: K2, with the left needle lift the right stitch on the right needle over the left stitch and off the needle, **K1, lift the right stitch over the left and off the needle. Repeat from ** three more times, binding off a total of four stitches. Slip the stitch from the right needle to the left needle.
5. Repeat steps 1–4.

Long-Chain Bind Off

Also called Crochet Bind Off, Crocheting Off

This bind off creates a series of chained loops along the edge. You can change the size of the loops by increasing or decreasing the number of chains. A crochet hook about the same size as the needle is required.

Long-chain bind off

1. Insert the hook into the first stitch as if to knit, wrap the yarn around the hook and pull a loop through the stitch, then *wrap the yarn around the hook and pull it through the loop on the hook five times. Drop the first stitch from the left needle.

2. Insert the hook through the next four stitches on the knitting needle from right to left, wrap the yarn around the hook and pull it through all four stitches.

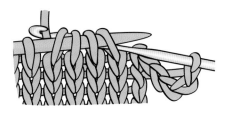

3. Wrap the yarn around the hook again and pull it through the two loops on the hook, sliding the four stitches off the knitting needle. Repeat from *.

Long-Chain Bind Off Variation

A variation of the long-chain bind off (at left), this technique also creates a series of chained loops.

1. Insert the hook into the first three stitches as if to knit. Wrap the yarn around the hook and pull it through the three stitches.

2. Make five chains by wrapping the yarn around the hook and pulling it through the stitch on the hook five times.

3. Insert the hook into the next three stitches on the left needle as if to knit. Wrap the yarn around the hook and pull the loop through the three stitches, then through the stitch on the hook.

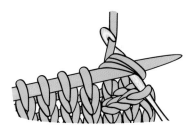

4. Repeat steps 2 and 3.

Increase Bind Offs

These bind offs lengthen and add elasticity to the edge by inserting stitches between the bound-off stitches. Some are useful for binding off lace work when the edge is scalloped, wavy, or heavily pointed. Others produce very stretchy edges good for ribbing, and are often used on toe-up socks for binding off the cuffs.

Frilled Bind Off

This bind off can be used with many bind offs to create a frilled edge. A stitch is added between the bound-off stitches to lengthen the edge and create the frill. Experiment with different bind offs to create your own special edge. Two examples are given here.

Frilled Standard Bind Off

Frilled standard bind off

1. K1, *knit the next stitch but keep the stitch on the left needle.

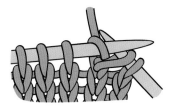

2. With the left needle, lift the right stitch on the right needle over the left stitch and off the needle.

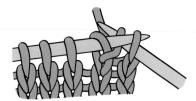

3. Knit the stitch on the left needle again and drop it off the left needle.

4. With the left needle, lift the right stitch over the left and off the needle; repeat from *.

Frilled Decrease Bind Off

Here the decrease bind off has an added stitch between those bound off.

Frilled decrease bind off

1. K1, *knit the next stitch, but keep the stitch on the left needle.
2. Slip the two stitches purlwise from the right to the left needle. K2tog through the back loops.

3. Slip the stitch purlwise from the right needle to the left. Knit the slipped stitch and the rest of the first stitch together through the back loops. Repeat from *.

Picot Chain Bind Off

Also called Yarn-Over Bind Off

This variation of the standard bind off (page 114) adds an extra stitch between the bound-off stitches, adding elasticity and length to the edge. It is particularly useful when binding off a scalloped or wavy lace edge. You can combine it with the standard bind off to vary the length of the edge: use the picot chain bind off where you need extra length and the standard bind off when you don't.

Picot chain bind off

1. Bind off one stitch using the standard bind off (page 114) as follows: K2, with the left needle tip lift the right stitch on the right needle over the left stitch and off the needle.

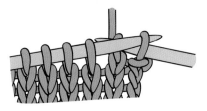

2. Insert the left needle into the front of the stitch on the right needle from left to right, wrap the working strand around the right needle as if to knit, lift the stitch on the left needle over the wrap and off the needle.

3. K1, lift the right stitch over the left and off the needle.

4. Repeat steps 2 and 3.

Sarah's Favorite Bind Off

Attributed to Sarah Hauschka, the next two bind offs involve inserting stitches to create a loose, slightly flared edge. A ratio of one backward loop (page 14) to four to six stitches works well.

Sarah's Favorite Bind Off for K1, P1 Rib

Sarah's favorite bind off for K1, P1 rib

1. K1, *make a backward loop and place it on the right needle.

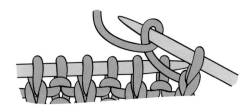

2. With the left needle, lift the right stitch on the right needle over the loop and off the needle.
3. P1, lift the right stitch over the loop and off the needle, K1, lift the right stitch over the left and off the needle. Repeat this step three to five more times. Repeat from *.

Sarah's Favorite Bind Off for K2, P2 Rib

Sarah's favorite bind off for K2, P2 rib

1. K1, make a backward loop and place it on the right needle.

2. With the left needle, lift the right stitch on the right needle over the loop and off the needle, K1, lift the right stitch over the left and off the needle, P1, lift the right stitch over the left and off the needle, P1, lift the right stitch over the left and off the needle.
3. Repeat steps 1 and 2.

Peggy's Stretchy Bind Off

Also called Stretchy Bind Off

This bind off from the Socknitters online group adds stitches in the row before the bind-off row. Because the added stitches are never knit, the edge is not as bulky as you might expect. Although needles one to two sizes larger than the project needles are called for, the project needles also work well.

Peggy's Stretchy Bind Off for K1, P1 Rib

Peggy's stretchy bind off for K1, P1 rib

1. On the row before binding off: *K1, make a backward loop (page 14) and place it on the right needle, P1; repeat from *.

2. Bind-off row: Using a larger right needle, K1, **slip the loop to the right needle as if to purl, lift the right stitch over the slipped loop and off the needle.
3. P1, with the left needle lift the right stitch on the right needle over the left stitch and off the needle, K1, lift the right stitch over the left and off the needle. Repeat from **.

Peggy's Stretchy Bind Off for K2, P2 Rib

Peggy's stretchy bind off for K2, P2 rib

1. On the row before binding off: *K2, make a backward loop (page 14) and place it on the right needle, P2, make a backward loop and place it on the needle; repeat from *, ending P2.

2. Bind-off row: Using a larger right needle, K2, with the left needle lift the right stitch on the right needle over the left stitch and off the needle.
3. **Slip the loop to the right needle as if to purl and lift the right stitch over the loop and off the needle, P1, lift the right stitch over the left stitch and off the needle, P1, lift the right stitch over the left and off the needle.
4. Slip the loop to the right needle as if to purl, lift the right stitch over the loop and off the needle, K1, lift the right stitch over the left stitch and off the needle, K1, lift the right stitch over the left stitch and off the needle. Repeat from **.

Peggy's Stretchy Bind Off for K2, P2 Rib Variation

This bind off is for K2, P2 ribbing in the round. Double yarn overs alternate with single yarn overs on either side of the two knit stitches to lengthen the edge.

Peggy's stretchy bind off for K2, P2 rib variation

1. On the row before binding off: *With the yarn in front, wrap the yarn counterclockwise around the right needle, ending with it on the front to make a double yarn over, K2, bring the yarn to the front and wrap the yarn counterclockwise around the right needle to make a yarn over, P2; repeat from * around.

2. Bind-off round: **Drop the first yarn over off the needle, insert the right needle into the next yarn over as if to purl.

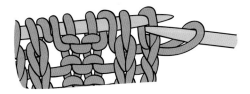

   Slip the loop to the right needle, K1, with the left needle lift the yarn over the left stitch and off the needle, K1, lift the right stitch over the left and off the needle.
3. Insert the right needle into the yarn over as if to purl and slip it to the right needle, with the left needle, lift the right stitch over the yarn over and off the needle, P1, lift the yarn over the left stitch and off the needle, P1, lift the right stitch over the left and off the needle. Repeat from **.

Yarn-Over Bind Off
Also called Modified Standard Bind Off

This bind off creates a decorative, open edge that is quite stretchy. The edge flares slightly, making it a good option for lace, ruffles, or sock cuffs. Once you learn this bind off, you can make the edge fit any scalloped or wavy pattern by varying the number and frequency of the yarn overs. Place more where the edge curves and fewer where the edge is straighter. Make a swatch to determine the best number and placement for a given pattern.

Yarn-over bind off

1. K1, bring the yarn to the front to make a yarn over, K1.

2. With the left needle, lift the yarn over (middle stitch) over the left stitch and off the needle, then lift the right stitch over the left stitch and off the needle.

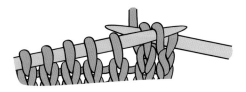

3. Bring the yarn to the front to make a yarn over, K1. Repeat steps 2 and 3.

Yarn-Over Bind Off Variation
Also called Modified Standard Bind Off

1. K2, with the left needle lift the right stitch on the right needle over the left stitch and off the needle.
2. Bring the yarn to the front to make a yarn over and K1.

3. Insert the left needle into both the yarn over and the right stitch on the right needle and lift them together over the left stitch and off the needle.

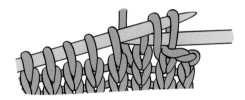

4. Repeat steps 2 and 3.

Jeny's Surprisingly Stretchy Bind Off

Also called JSSB

Jeny Staiman's variation of the standard bind off creates a very elastic edge for K1, P1 ribbing that is well suited to hats, neckbands, and sock cuffs. The yarn over creates a more open edge than some other bind offs.

Jeny's surprisingly stretchy bind off

1. Wrap the yarn clockwise around the right needle to make a reverse yarn over.

2. K1, with the left needle, lift the yarn-over loop over the knit stitch and off the needle.

3. Bring the yarn to the front and wrap it around the right needle counterclockwise to make a yarn over.

4. P1, with the left needle lift the yarn-over loop over the purl stitch and off the needle, then lift the right stitch over the left stitch and off the needle.
5. Wrap the yarn clockwise around the right needle to make a reverse yarn over, K1, with the left needle lift the yarn-over loop over the knit stitch and off the needle, then lift the right stitch over the left stitch and off the needle.

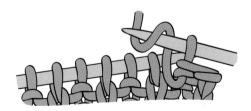

6. Bring the yarn to the front and wrap it around the right needle counterclockwise to make a yarn over, P1, lift the yarn-over loop over the purl stitch and off the needle, then lift the right stitch over the left stitch and off the needle.
7. Repeat steps 5 and 6.

Special Bind Offs

This is a miscellaneous group of bind offs that have special applications, such as joining two pieces while binding them off, closing up circular work, and shaping garments.

Slanted Bind Off

Also called Stepped Bind Off, Sloped Bind Off, Diagonal Bind Off, Bias Bind Off

This bind off creates a smooth rather than stepped edge when binding off several groups of stitches along the same side. It's useful when shaping shoulders or sleeve caps.

Slanted bind off

1. Bind off the first group of stitches and work to the end. On the next row, work to the last stitch on the left needle and turn the work.

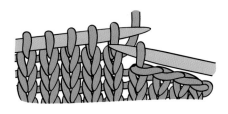

2. The unworked stitch will be on the right needle. Slip the first stitch on the left needle purlwise to the right needle.

3. With the left needle, lift the unworked stitch over the left stitch and off the needle as the first bound-off stitch in the second group. Continue to bind off the rest of the stitches in the second group normally. Repeat from step 1 for each additional group of stitches to be bound off.

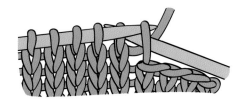

Slanted Bind Off Variation

Follow directions for the slanted bind off (at left), but for step 2, work the first stitch and then lift the unworked stitch over it for the first bound-off stitch.

Japanese Bind Off

Also called Japanese Three-Needle Bind Off

This bind off closes up circular knitting and creates a flatter seam than the standard three-needle bind off. It combines the stitches from several needles onto one so that they can be bound off. You will need three needles, or two needles and a crochet hook.

Japanese bind off

1. Place the stitches evenly on two needles and hold the needles parallel to each other with wrong sides together.

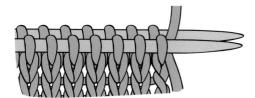

2. Insert a third needle (or hook) through the first stitch on the front needle as if to knit and through the first stitch on the back needle as if to purl.

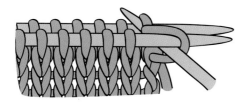

3. Pull the stitch on the back needle through the stitch on the front needle and drop both stitches off the front needle.
4. Repeat steps 2 and 3. The opening is now closed with all the stitches on the right needle. If you used a hook, transfer the stitches to a needle. Bind off using any method you wish.

Three-Needle Bind Off

Also called Knitted Bind Off, Seam Bind Off, Joinery Bind Off

This bind off joins two pieces while binding them off. It creates a strong, firm seam particularly good for shoulders.

If the right sides face each other, the seam will be hidden on the inside of the garment. If wrong sides face each other, the seam will create a neat, decorative ridge. The two sides of the ridge are different, so to make them look alike on a garment, work one shoulder seam from right to left and the other from left to right.

Three-needle bind off, right sides together

Three-needle bind off, wrong sides together

1. With the two pieces of knitting to be joined still on the needles, place them with their right sides (or wrong sides) facing and the needles parallel and pointing to the right. Insert a third needle into the first stitch on each needle and knit the two stitches together using one of the working strands.

2. Knit the next stitch on each needle as in step 1.
3. With one of the left needles, lift the right stitch on the right needle over the left stitch and off the needle.

4. Repeat steps 2 and 3.

BIND OFFS

Three-Needle I-Cord Bind Off

Also called Seam Bind Off

This variation of the three-needle bind off (page 137) creates an I-cord along the seam. Vary the width of the I-cord by increasing or decreasing the number of I-cord stitches.

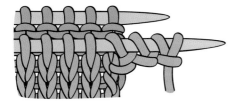

Three-needle I-cord bind off

1. With the right side of one of the pieces to be bound off facing you, cast on three stitches using the knit cast on (page 48) as follows: *Knit the first stitch. Rotate the right needle clockwise, insert the tip of the left needle into the stitch from left to right and remove the right needle; repeat from * two more times. These three stitches are the I-cord stitches.

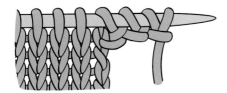

2. Place together the two pieces to be bound off, wrong sides facing, with the one with the three I-cord stitches in front. The needles will be parallel with their tips pointing to the right.

3. With a third needle, knit two I-cord stitches and slip the third to the right needle as if to purl.

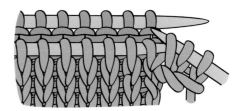

4. Insert the right needle into the first stitch on each needle and knit the two stitches together.

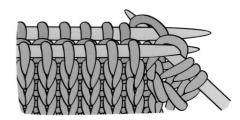

5. With one of the left needles, lift the second stitch in from the needle tip over the stitch closest to the tip and off the needle. Place the front left needle and the right needle tips together and slip the three I-cord stitches back to the front left needle.

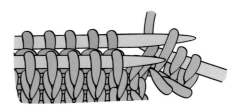

6. Repeat steps 3–5 until only the I-cord stitches remain. Lift the middle stitch over the left stitch and off the needle. Then lift the right stitch over the left and off the needle.

Russian Grafting

This technique binds off stitches while joining two pieces, producing a decorative zigzag seam along the edge. It doesn't require more yarn and produces a tight, strong seam.

Russian grafting

1. Distribute the stitches evenly on two needles. With the right sides facing you, hold one needle in each hand with the tips pointing toward each other and the working strands on the outside edges.

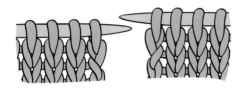

2. Place the needle tips together and slip the first stitch on the right needle to the left needle.

3. With the right needle, lift the second stitch on the left needle over the first stitch and off the needle.

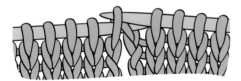

4. Insert the right needle into the first stitch on the left needle as if to purl, then into the second stitch as if to knit, and then pull the second stitch through the first stitch, dropping both from the left needle.

5. Place the needle tips together and slip the first two stitches on the right needle to the left needle.

6. With the right needle, lift the second stitch on the left needle over the first stitch and off the needle.

7. Repeat steps 4–6 until two stitches remain. Place the needle tips together and slip the stitch on the right needle to the left needle. With the right needle, lift the left stitch on the left needle over the right stitch and off the needle.

Russian Grafting Variation

This version is more awkward, but it creates the same seam.

1. Set up as in step 1 of Russian grafting (page 139).

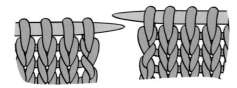

2. Place the needle tips together and slip the first stitch on the right needle to the left needle.

3. Insert the right needle into the first stitch on the left needle as if to purl, then into the second stitch as if to knit, and then pull the second stitch through the first stitch, dropping both off the left needle.

4. Insert the left needle into the first stitch on the right needle from left to right so that the tip sticks out in back.

5. Insert the left needle into the second stitch from behind (back to front) and pull the stitch through the first stitch, dropping them both off the right needle.

6. Repeat steps 3–5.

Russian Grafting with Crochet Hook

This method uses a crochet hook to produce the same zigzag seam as Russian grafting (page 139).

Russian grafting with crochet hook

1. Distribute the stitches evenly on two needles. Hold the needles parallel to each other with the wrong sides facing and the working strands on the left.

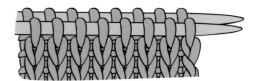

2. Insert the hook into the first stitch on the back needle as if to knit and slip the stitch to the hook.

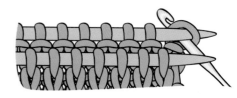

3. Insert the hook into the first stitch on the front needle as if to knit and slip the stitch to the hook.

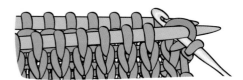

4. Pull the left stitch through the right stitch.

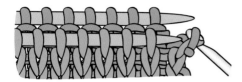

5. Insert the hook into the first stitch on the back needle as if to knit, slip the stitch to the hook, and pull the left stitch through the right stitch.

6. Repeat steps 3–5 until one stitch remains. Break the yarn and pull the tail through the last stitch.

Zigzag Bind Off

Priscilla Gibson Roberts found this bind off joining the heel flaps on a pair of historic Greek socks. Joining two pieces with a zigzag chain along the seam, it forms a less bulky seam than the three-needle bind off (page 137) and works nicely for joining the toes of socks or heel flaps. It requires three needles.

Zigzag bind off

1. Distribute the stitches evenly on two needles. Place the needles parallel to each other with the wrong sides facing. Using a third needle and the front working strand, P1 on the back needle.

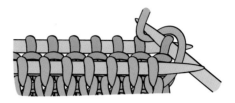

2. K1 on the front needle, with a left needle lift the right (purl) stitch over the left (knit) stitch and off the needle.

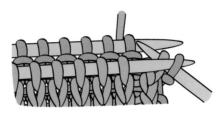

3. P1 on the back needle, with the left needle lift the right (knit) stitch over the left (purl) stitch and off needle.

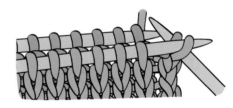

4. Repeat steps 2 and 3.

Cowichan Double Bind Off

The Cowichan, a group of the Coast Salish people of British Columbia, use this technique to join shoulders while binding them off. It creates a firm edge with two parallel chains along it and seamless stockinette stitch on the reverse. It requires three needles, one of which is double-pointed—ideally a short cable needle. When you rotate the cable needle, keep the working strand to the left of the needle. Priscilla Gibson Roberts introduced this bind off to the larger knitting community.

Cowichan double bind off

1. Finish both pieces with a wrong-side row. Distribute the stitches evenly on two needles. Place the needles parallel to each other with the wrong sides facing.

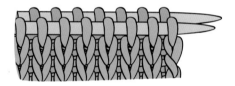

2. With the cable needle, knit the first stitch on the front needle using the front working strand.

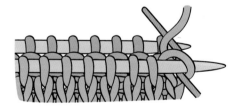

3. Rotate the cable needle counterclockwise so that the tip that was closest to you is now in the back.

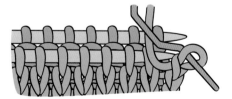

4. With the cable needle, purl the first stitch on the back needle, using the same working strand.

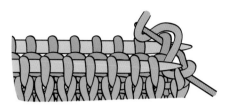

5. Rotate the needle back clockwise to its original position.

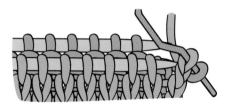

6. Knit the next stitch on the front needle.

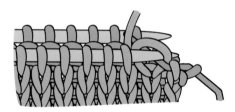

7. With the front left needle, lift the middle stitch on the cable needle over the left stitch and off the needle, binding off one stitch on the front.

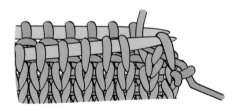

8. Rotate the cable needle counterclockwise to the back and P1.
9. With the front left needle, lift the middle stitch on the cable needle over the left stitch and off the needle, binding off one stitch on the back.
10. Rotate the cable needle back clockwise to its original position.
11. Repeat steps 6–10, alternating binding off from the front and back needles until one stitch remains on each needle. Knit the two stitches together.

BIND OFFS

Sewn Bind Offs

The techniques in this group use tapestry needles to bind off the stitches. Although you may find these bind offs slow and cumbersome, you will be pleased by their neat, flexible edges. The edges are also thinner and less visible than bind offs using knitting needles.

The yarn you choose may determine whether or not these are appropriate for use with a particular project. Since the yarn will be pulled through every bind-off stitch you make, soft yarns will fray if there are many stitches to bind off. Likewise, textured yarns or yarns with mohair or other long fibers may catch as the yarn is pulled through, making the bind off difficult.

It takes practice to pull the yarn through the stitches with just the right tension. The yarn should be snug, but not too tight or the edge will pucker. The tension should match that of your knitting. As you work these bind offs, be careful not to split a stitch with the needle.

Simple Bind Off

Also called Provisional Bind Off, Stranded Bind Off, Heart of Blossom Bind Off

This is the simplest way to remove stitches from the needle. When knitting flat, the tightness of the edge can be easily adjusted. For circular knitting, it's a good way to finish toes, fingers, mittens, I-cords, and hat crowns.

Simple Bind Off for Flat Knitting

What could be simpler than this?

Simple bind off for flat knitting

Break the yarn, leaving a tail about 5" longer than the width of the edge to be bound off, and thread it onto a yarn needle. Thread the needle through the stitches on the knitting needle, pull the yarn through, and remove the needle. Knot the end around the last stitch and remove the needle.

Simple Bind Off for Circular Knitting

Also called Heart of Blossom Bind Off

This bind off works best with a small number of stitches.

Simple bind off for circular knitting

1. Break the yarn, leaving a tail several inches longer than the edge being bound off, and thread it onto a yarn needle. Slip the needle through the stitches on the knitting needle and remove the knitting needle.
2. Pull the yarn to close the hole, and fasten the end on the inside.

Double-Stranded Bind Off

Also called Sande's Stretchy Bind Off

Because each stitch is wrapped twice, this bind off creates a firm edge. It can be used to close toes, fingers, and other round elements.

Double-stranded bind off

1. Break the yarn, leaving a tail two to three times the width of the edge to be bound off, and thread it onto a yarn needle. *Insert the needle through the first two stitches as if to purl.

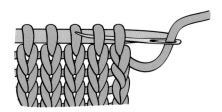

2. Pull the yarn through and drop the first stitch off the needle; repeat from *.

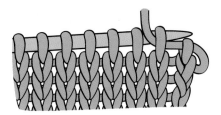

Sewn Bind Off

Also called Backstitch Bind Off, Cast-On Bind Off

Elizabeth Zimmerman called this the most elastic bind off she knew. While not good for ribbing, it is excellent for garter and stockinette stitches, as well as necklines and sock cuffs, where elasticity is important. Pair it with the long-tail cast on (page 18) if you would like matching edges.

Sewn bind off

1. Break the yarn, leaving a tail three times the width of the edge to be bound off, and thread it onto a yarn needle. *Insert the needle through the first two stitches as if to purl, and pull the yarn through.

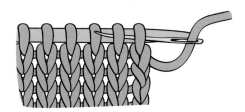

2. Insert the needle through the first stitch as if to knit, pull the yarn through, and slip the stitch off the needle. Repeat from *.

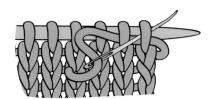

BIND OFFS

Latvian Bind Off

This bind off from Joyce Williams produces a decorative edge that is quite flexible.

Latvian bind off

1. Break the yarn, leaving a tail about three times the width of the edge to be bound off, and thread it onto a yarn needle. Insert the needle from back to front through the first stitch on the needle, and pull the yarn through.

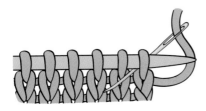

2. Move two stitches to the left, insert the needle through the stitch from front to back, and pull the yarn through.

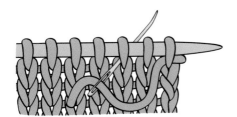

3. Insert the needle into the next stitch to the right from back to front, making sure the needle passes under the horizontal strand just made, and pull the yarn through.

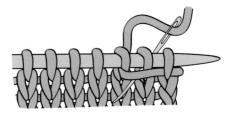

4. Move two stitches to the left, insert the needle through the stitch from front to back, and pull the yarn through.

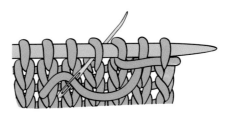

5. Insert the needle into the next stitch to the right from back to front, making sure the needle passes above the horizontal strand just made.

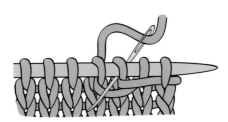

6. Repeat steps 2–5 until all stitches have been worked. Remove the knitting needle, slide the horizontal strands up to the top of the edge, and adjust the tension of the stitches if necessary.

Stem-Stitch Bind Off

Also called Sewn Bind Off, Half-Hitch Bind Off, Outline-Stitch Bind Off

This bind off creates an edge very similar to the long-tail cast on (page 18), with slanted strands on the front and bumps on the back. It can be worked on either the right side or the wrong side of your project.

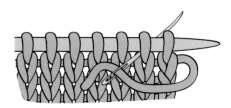

Stem stitch bind off

1. Break the yarn, leaving a tail about four times the width of the edge to be bound off, and thread it onto a yarn needle. *Insert the needle into the second stitch from front to back, and pull the yarn through.

2. Insert the needle into the first stitch from back to front, going under the horizontal strand just made. Pull the yarn through and drop the first stitch from the knitting needle. Repeat from *.

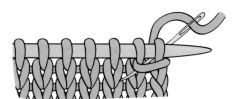

Stem-Stitch Bind Off: Opposite Slant Variation

Also called Invisible Sewn Bind Off

This variation slants the strands in the opposite direction.

Stem-stitch bind off: opposite slant variation

Follow the steps for the stem-stitch bind off (at left), except when inserting the needle into the next stitch to the right from back to front, make sure the needle passes over the horizontal strand just made.

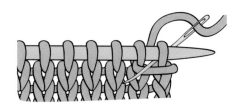

Stem-Stitch Bind Off: Reverse Variation

This variation from Joyce Williams is the reverse of the stem-stitch bind off (at left), with the bumps on the front and the slanting strands on the back.

Stem-stitch bind off: reverse variation

1. Break the yarn, leaving a tail about three times the width of the edge to be bound off, and thread it onto a yarn needle. Insert the needle through the second stitch on the needle from back to front, and pull the yarn through.

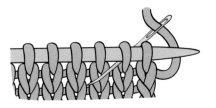

2. Insert the needle through the next stitch to the right from front to back, and pull the yarn through.

3. Move two stitches to the left, insert the needle into the stitch from back to front, and pull the yarn through.

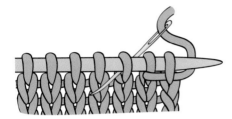

4. Insert the needle into the stitch immediately to the right from front to back, making sure the needle passes over the horizontal strand just made in back.

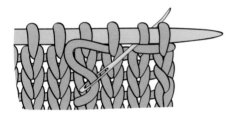

5. Repeat steps 3 and 4 until all stitches have been worked. Remove the knitting needle and adjust the tension of the stitches if necessary.

Loop Bind Off

Featuring a series of loops across the edge, this matches the loop cast on. You may find it easier to maintain the tension by keeping the stitches on the needle until you've finished binding off.

Loop bind off

1. Break the yarn, leaving a tail three to four times the width of the edge to be bound off, and thread it onto a yarn needle. Insert the needle into the first stitch from front to back, pull the yarn through, and slip the stitch off the needle.

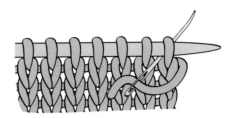

2. With the yarn above your work, insert the needle into the next stitch on the needle from front to back, then into the dropped stitch from back to front, pull the yarn through, and slip the stitch from the left needle. Repeat this step.

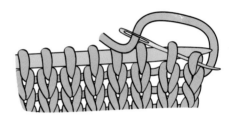

Loop Bind Off Variation

Also called Outline-Stitch Bind Off, Casting-On Cast Off
This variation is worked from left to right.

1. End with a right-side row. Break the yarn, leaving a tail about three times the width of the edge to be bound off, and thread it onto a yarn needle.
2. With the right side facing you and the yarn above the needle, insert the needle into the second stitch in from the needle tip from front to back, then into the end stitch from back to front, pull the yarn through, and drop the end stitch from the needle. Repeat this step.

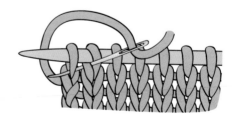

Kitchener Stitch

Also called Grafting

This technique joins two pieces of knitting seamlessly. It's commonly used to join toe stitches when knitting socks from the cuff down, but you can turn to it whenever you want to join two pieces seamlessly with live stitches. It's most effective with stockinette and garter stitches, but you can use it for pattern stitches as well. It can be worked with the stitches on or off the needles. When moving between needles, bring the yarn under the needle tips on the right.

Kitchener stitch for stockinette stitch;
the white stitches are the sewn ones

Kitchener Stitch for
Stockinette Stitch (on Needles)

1. End one piece with a right-side row. Break the yarn, leaving a long tail, and thread it onto a yarn needle. Hold the two needles parallel to each other with the wrong sides facing and with the working strand on the right of the back needle. Insert the needle into the first stitch on the front needle as if to purl, and then into the first stitch on the back needle as if to knit.

2. Insert the needle into the first stitch on the front needle as if to knit, pull the yarn through, and drop the stitch from the knitting needle.

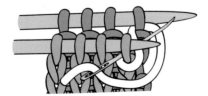

3. Insert the needle into the next stitch on the front needle as if to purl, and pull the yarn through.

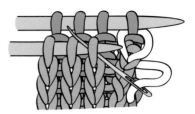

4. Insert the needle into the first stitch on the back needle as if to purl, pull the yarn through, and drop the stitch from the knitting needle.

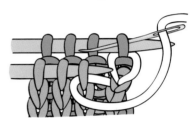

5. Insert the needle into the next stitch on the back needle as if to knit, and pull the yarn through.

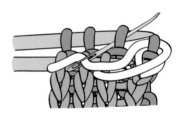

6. Repeat steps 2–5.

Kitchener Stitch for
Stockinette Stitch (off Needles)

1. Break the yarn, leaving a long tail, and thread it onto a yarn needle. Place the two pieces to be joined on a flat surface with right sides facing up and the needles next to and parallel to each other, with the pieces extending away from each other. The yarn tail is on the right end of the upper piece. Carefully remove the knitting needles. Insert the needle into the first stitch on the lower piece from back to front and pull the yarn through. Then insert the needle into the first stitch on the upper piece from back to front and pull the yarn through.

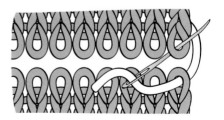

2. Insert the needle into the already worked stitch on the lower piece from front to back, then into the next stitch from back to front, and pull the yarn through.

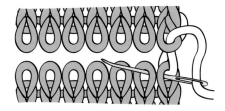

3. Insert the needle into the stitch already worked on the upper piece from front to back, then into the next stitch from back to front, and pull the yarn through.

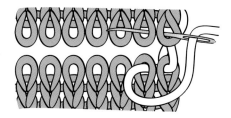

4. Repeat steps 2 and 3.

Kitchener Stitch for Garter Stitch

Kitchener stitch for garter stitch; the white stitches are the sewn ones

Kitchener Stitch for Garter Stitch (on Needles)

1. Set up as in step 1 of Kitchener stitch for stockinette stitch (on needles) opposite, with the knit side (of the last row) of the front needle facing the purl side of the back needle and the working strand on the right of the back needle. Insert the needle into the first stitch on the front needle as if to purl, and pull the yarn through. Then insert the needle into the

first stitch on the back needle as if to purl, and pull the yarn through.

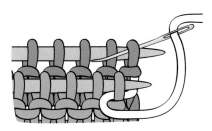

2. Insert the needle into the first stitch on the front needle as if to knit. Pull the yarn through and slip the stitch off the needle.

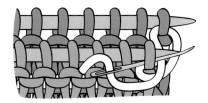

3. Insert the needle into the next stitch on the front needle as if to purl and pull the yarn through, leaving the stitch on the knitting needle.

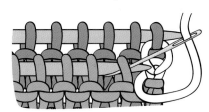

4. Insert the needle into the first stitch on the back needle as if to knit, pull the yarn through, and slip the stitch off the knitting needle.

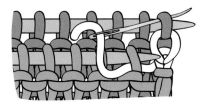

5. Insert the needle into the next stitch on the back needle as if to purl and pull the yarn through, leaving the stitch on the knitting needle.

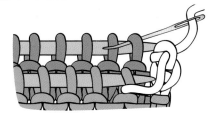

6. Repeat steps 2–5.

Kitchener Stitch for Garter Stitch (off Needles)

1. Set up as in step 1 of Kitchener stitch for stockinette stitch (off needles) (page 148) with the knit side (of the last row) of the top needle facing up and the purl side of the lower needle facing up. Follow the steps for the Kitchener stitch for garter stitch (on needles) (page 149) without dropping the stitches off the knitting needles.

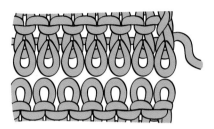

2. Insert the needle into the first stitch on the lower piece from back to front, and pull the yarn through.
3. Insert the needle into the first stitch on the upper piece from front to back, and pull the yarn through.
4. Insert the needle into the already worked stitch on the lower piece from front to back, then into the next stitch from back to front, and pull the yarn through.
5. Insert the needle into the already worked stitch on the upper piece from back to front, then into the next stitch from front to back, and pull the yarn through.
6. Repeat steps 4 and 5.

Tubular Bind Offs

These bind offs are all very similar and create the same edge: neat and rounded. The edges are very strong and elastic and are mainly used for ribbing, although some knitters like them for the brioche stitch as well. They can be paired with tubular cast ons (page 75) for matching edges.

These bind offs are often confused with sewn bind offs. Although they require a yarn needle, they create the rounded tubular edge that the sewn bind offs do not.

Several of the tubular bind offs involve double knitting to help create the rounded edge. See the note about double knitting in the introduction to tubular cast ons (page 75). As you work these bind offs, be careful not to split stitches with the needle.

Tubular Bind Off

This bind off creates a stretchy edge that is well suited to tight necks or other constricted edges where elasticity is required. It involves double knitting.

Tubular bind off

1. For the last two to four rows, change to double knitting.
   Working flat:
   *K1, slip 1 purlwise with yarn in front; repeat from *.
   Repeat the last row.

Working in the round:

Round 1: *K1, slip 1 purlwise with yarn in front; repeat from *.

Round 2: *Slip 1 purlwise with yarn in back, P1; repeat from *.

Repeat rounds 1 and 2.

2. Break the yarn, leaving a long tail, and thread it onto a yarn needle. Carefully pull out the knitting needles. The stitches will separate, with the knit stitches falling to the front and the purl stitches to the back.

3. Place the knit stitches on one knitting needle and the purl stitches on another. Weave the stitches together using the Kitchener stitch.

Kitchener Bind Off

Also called Invisible Weave Off, Tubular Bind Off, Italian Bind Off, Binding Off in Kitchener Rib

This is the Kitchener stitch (page 148) worked on one needle for K1, P1 ribbing, but it can also be used with the brioche stitch. Its variation involves double knitting. Both are often worked on needles two sizes smaller than the project needle for the last few rows.

Kitchener bind off

1. Break the yarn, leaving a tail about three times the width of the edge to be bound off, and thread it onto a yarn needle. *Insert the needle into the first (knit) stitch as if to knit, pull the yarn through, and slip the stitch off the needle.

2. Insert the needle into the second knit stitch as if to purl, and pull the yarn through.

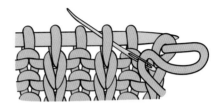

3. With the needle in back, insert the needle into the first stitch (purl) on the needle as if to purl. Pull the yarn through and slip the stitch off the needle.

4. With the needle in back, insert it into the next (purl) stitch on the needle as if to knit, and pull the yarn through.

5. Repeat from *.

Kitchener Bind Off Variation

Also called Italian Bind Off, Binding Off in Kitchener Rib

This variation starts the bind off with double knitting.

Kitchener bind off variation

1. For the last two rows, change to double knitting.
   Working flat:
   *K1, slip 1 purlwise with yarn in front; repeat from *.
   Repeat last row.

   Working in the round:
   Round 1: *K1, slip 1 purlwise with yarn in front; repeat from *.
   Round 2: *Slip 1 purlwise with yarn in back, P1; repeat from *.
   Repeat rounds 1 and 2.
2. Cut the yarn, leaving a tail three to four times the length of the edge to be bound off, and thread it onto a yarn needle. Then follow steps 1–4 of the Kitchener bind off (page 151).

Kitchener Double-Rib Bind Off

This bind-off method for K2, P2 ribbing requires double-pointed needles.

Kitchener double-rib bind off

1. Break the yarn, leaving a tail about three times the length of the edge to be bound off, and thread it onto a yarn needle.
2. Place the purl stitches on one needle and the knit stitches on another needle. Hold the needles parallel, with the knit stitches on the front needle.

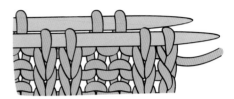

3. Insert the needle into the first knit stitch as if to purl, and pull the yarn through.

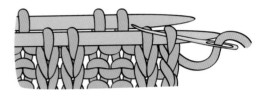

4. Insert the needle into the first purl stitch as if to knit, and pull the yarn through.

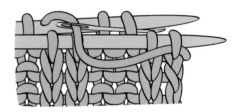

5. Bring the needle to the front and insert it into the first knit stitch as if to knit, pull the yarn through, and drop the stitch off the needle.

6. Insert the needle into the next knit stitch as if to purl, and pull the yarn through.

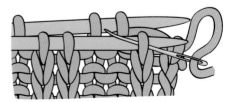

BIND OFFS

7. Insert the needle into the first purl stitch as if to purl, pull the yarn through, and drop the stitch off the needle.

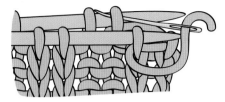

8. Insert the needle into the next purl stitch as if to knit, and pull the yarn through.

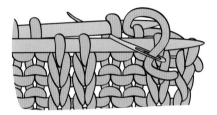

9. Repeat steps 5–8.

Invisible Ribbed Bind Off

Also called Invisible Bind Off, K1, P1 Bind Off, K1, P1 Rib Bind Off, Italian Bind Off, Kitchener Rib Bind Off, Kitchener Bind Off, Tubular Bind Off

This method is for K1, P1 ribbing, but it also works well with the brioche stitch.

Invisible ribbed bind off

Invisible Ribbed Bind Off (on Needles)

1. Break the yarn, leaving a tail about three times the width of the piece to be bound off, and thread it onto a yarn needle. Insert the needle into the first knit stitch as if to purl, and pull the yarn through.

2. Bring the needle behind the knit stitch, and insert it into the second (purl) stitch from front to back as if to knit. Pull the yarn through and bring the needle to the front.

3. Insert the needle into the first knit stitch as if to knit, and drop the stitch off the knitting needle.

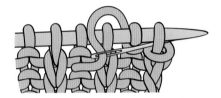

4. Insert the needle into the next knit stitch as if to purl, and pull the yarn through.

5. Insert the needle into the first (purl) stitch as if to purl, and drop the stitch off the knitting needle.

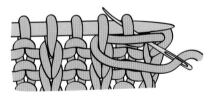

6. Bring the needle behind the first stitch on the knitting needle and insert into the next purl stitch from front to back. Pull the yarn through.

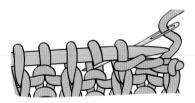

7. Repeat steps 3–6. End by inserting the needle into the last knit stitch as if to knit and dropping it off the knitting needle, inserting the needle into the last stitch as if to purl and dropping it off the needle; pull the yarn tight.

Invisible Ribbed Bind Off (off Needles)

1. Break the yarn, leaving a tail about three times the width of the edge to be bound off, and thread it onto a yarn needle. Place the work face up on a table, with the working strand on the right side. Carefully remove the needle.

2. Insert the needle into the first knit stitch from back to front, then into the first purl stitch from front to back, and pull the yarn through.

3. Insert the needle into the just-worked knit stitch from front to back, then into the next knit stitch from back to front, and pull the yarn through.

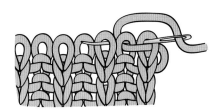

4. Insert the needle into the just-worked purl stitch from back to front, then into the next purl stitch from front to back, and pull the yarn through.

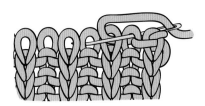

5. Repeat steps 3 and 4 until the needle has gone through the last purl stitch once. Insert the needle into the just-worked knit stitch from front to back, then into the last purl stitch from back to front.

Invisible Double-Rib Bind Off

This bind off is for K2, P2 ribbing.

Invisible double-rib bind off

1. Cut the yarn, leaving a tail three times the width of the edge to be bound off, and thread it onto a yarn needle. Insert the needle into the first (knit) stitch as if to purl, and pull the yarn through.

2. Bring the needle behind the first two knit stitches, insert it into the first purl stitch from front to back, and pull the yarn through.

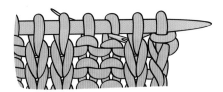

3. Insert the needle into the first knit stitch as if to knit, and drop the stitch off the needle.

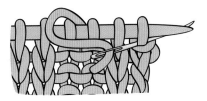

4. Insert the needle into the second knit stitch as if to purl, and pull the yarn through.

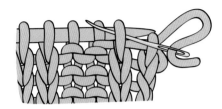

5. Bring the needle behind the knit stitch, insert it into the first purl stitch from back to front, and pull the yarn through.

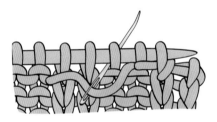

6. Insert the needle into the second purl stitch as if to knit, and pull the yarn through.

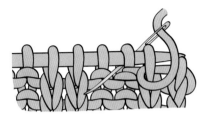

7. Insert the needle into the first knit stitch as if to knit, and drop the stitch off the needle.

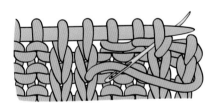

8. Insert the needle into the next knit stitch as if to purl, and drop the first purl stitch off the knitting needle.

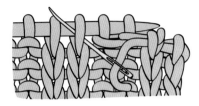

9. Insert the needle into the first purl stitch as if to purl, pull the yarn through, and drop the stitch off the needle.

10. Bring the needle behind the next two knit stitches, insert it into the next purl stitch from front to back, and pull the yarn through.

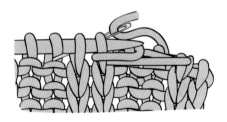

11. Repeat steps 3–10, ending with steps 5 and 6 for the last two purl stitches.

Acknowledgments

Many people have played an important role in the production of this book and I am most grateful to them all. My thanks go to:

Claire Wilson for first putting me on to cast ons and bind offs, suggesting them as a topic for me to teach at a Green Mountain Spinnery Knitters' Weekend. Who could have predicted then that it would go this far?!

Margaret Atkinson, Maureen Clark, Melissa Johnson, and Eric Robinson of the Spinnery's product development department for believing in this project from the very beginning. They have been extremely supportive and have done everything in their power to promote this endeavor and speed it into being.

The Green Mountain Spinnery for generously supplying all the yarn for the swatches.

Lynne Barr, Judy Becker, Cat Bordhi, Rita Buchanan, Nancy Bush, Sara Hauschka, Mary Hu, Mary Scott Huff, Kerrie James, Mary Johnson, Wendy Johnson, Janet Rehfeldt, Priscilla Gibson Roberts, Iris Schreier, Charlene Schurch, Jeny Staiman, Montse Stanley, Patti Pierce Stone, and Joyce Williams for sharing their cast ons.

Gudrun Johnston, Sharon Miller, and Rhoda Hughson for information about casting on in Shetland.

The First Monday Knitters, especially Denise Acampora, Julia Bogardus, Lynn Street, and Patti Garland, for helping in numerous ways to bring this book to life, especially for testing directions.

My sister, Ann Monoyios, for her willingness to jump through enormous hoops to help this book come into being.

Everyone at Martingale, especially my technical editor, Ursula Reikes. They all worked hard to make this book better than I could have done alone.

Libby Mills, who has believed in me and unconditionally supported all my efforts, not just this book, for more years than seems possible.

And David, who has lived through every stage of the production of this book, tirelessly offering help and support.

About the Author

An avid knitter, Cap Sease has been knitting since childhood, having learned from her grandmother. She is also a weaver, quilter, and basket maker. Her love of using her hands led to a career in art conservation, working with archaeological and ethnographic objects.

She has worked primarily in museums, but she also has extensive experience as a conservator on archaeological excavations in the Mediterranean and Middle East. Since 2005 Cap has been a designer for the Green Mountain Spinnery and has taught workshops on various techniques, including cast ons and bind offs, for their Knitters' Weekends. She lives in Connecticut with her husband, David.

Photo ©Gale Zucker/www.gzucker.com

What's your creative passion?
Find it at ShopMartingale.com

books • eBooks • ePatterns • daily blog • free projects
videos • tutorials • inspiration • giveaways

Martingale®
Create with Confidence

Index